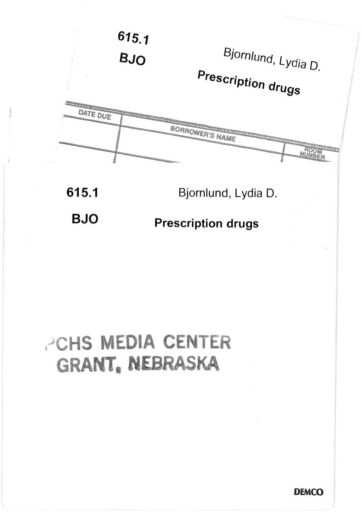

615.1

BJO

Bjornlund, Lydia D.

Prescription drugs

DATE DUE	BORROWER'S NAME	ROOM NUMBER

Prescription Drugs

by Lydia Bjornlund

Current Issues

ReferencePoint Press™

San Diego, CA

ReferencePoint
Press™

© 2009 ReferencePoint Press, Inc.

For more information, contact:
ReferencePoint Press, Inc.
PO Box 27779
San Diego, CA 92198
www.ReferencePointPress.com

Picture credits:
Maury Aaseng: 34–37, 53–55, 70–73, 90–93
AP Images: 11, 17

Bjornlund, Lydia
   Prescription drugs/by Lydia Bjornlund.
     p. cm.—(Compact research)
   Includes bibliographical references and index.
   ISBN-13: 978-1-60152-046-3 (hardback)
   ISBN-10: 1-60152-046-8 (hardback)
   1. Drugs—Popular works. 2. Drug abuse. 3. Pharmaceutical industry. I. Title.
   RM122.5.B56 2008
   615'1—dc22
                                                 2008025203

Contents

Foreword

As modern civilization continues to evolve, its ability to create, store, distribute, and access information expands exponentially. The explosion of information from all media continues to increase at a phenomenal rate. By 2020 some experts predict the worldwide information base will double every 73 days. While access to diverse sources of information and perspectives is paramount to any democratic society, information alone cannot help people gain knowledge and understanding. Information must be organized and presented clearly and succinctly in order to be understood. The challenge in the digital age becomes not the creation of information, but how best to sort, organize, enhance, and present information.

ReferencePoint Press developed the *Compact Research* series with this challenge of the information age in mind. More than any other subject area today, researching current issues can yield vast, diverse, and unqualified information that can be intimidating and overwhelming for even the most advanced and motivated researcher. The *Compact Research* series offers a compact, relevant, intelligent, and conveniently organized collection of information covering a variety of current topics ranging from illegal immigration and methamphetamine to diseases such as anorexia and meningitis.

The series focuses on three types of information: objective single-author narratives, opinion-based primary source quotations, and facts and statistics. The clearly written objective narratives provide context and reliable background information. Primary source quotes are carefully selected and cited, exposing the reader to differing points of view. And facts and statistics sections aid the reader in evaluating perspectives. Presenting these key types of information creates a richer, more balanced learning experience.

For better understanding and convenience, the series enhances information by organizing it into narrower topics and adding design features that make it easy for a reader to identify desired content. For example, in *Compact Research: Illegal Immigration*, a chapter covering the economic impact of illegal immigration has an objective narrative explaining the various ways the economy is impacted, a balanced section of numerous primary source quotes on the topic, followed by facts and full-color illustrations to encourage evaluation of contrasting perspectives.

The ancient Roman philosopher Lucius Annaeus Seneca wrote, "It is quality rather than quantity that matters." More than just a collection of content, the *Compact Research* series is simply committed to creating, finding, organizing, and presenting the most relevant and appropriate amount of information on a current topic in a user-friendly style that invites, intrigues, and fosters understanding.

Prescription Drugs at a Glance

Prevalence

Over 50 percent of Americans take at least one prescription medication daily, and 19 percent are taking four or more prescription drugs.

Common Prescription Drugs

The most widely prescribed categories of drugs include those used to treat high cholesterol, ulcers and other stomach problems, and mental illness.

Costs

In 2007 Americans spent almost $208.7 billion on prescription drugs. This is more than five times as much as in 1990, when the bill for prescription drugs was $40.3 billion.

Benefits

Prescription drugs save countless lives. Drugs that treat high blood pressure and high cholesterol reduce the risk of stroke and heart attack by as much as 30 percent; antibiotics have drastically reduced the number of deaths due to an infection; AIDS and cancer medications postpone the progression of these diseases.

Advertising

Drug companies spent over $4.4 billion on direct-to-consumer advertising to convince people of the benefits of their products.

Safety

The U.S. Food and Drug Administration (FDA) is responsible for approving all proposed drugs before they can be marketed and monitoring the drugs already on the market.

Adverse Effects

Some prescription drugs have serious risks, which increase when the drug is used for a purpose other than intended and/or when taken in combination with other drugs.

Abuse

Over 20 percent of Americans have used prescription medications for nonmedical purposes at some point in their lives.

Law Enforcement

The abuse of prescription drugs is governed by the Controlled Substances Act, which was passed as part of the Comprehensive Drug Abuse and Control Act of 1970. The Controlled Substances Act controls the use of five classes of drugs: narcotics, CNS depressants, stimulants, hallucinogens and anabolic steroids.

Health Dangers

When abused, prescription drugs pose a range of health dangers, including addiction and death from accidental poisoning.

Overview

66 **Drugs have brought tremendous benefits: preventing hospitalizations, eliminating surgeries, or getting a patient out of an institution. And even more important are the benefits of these medicines in terms of saved lives, reduced suffering, and more productive and fulfilling lives.** 99

—Scott Gottlieb, Speech at the Thirtieth International Good Manufacturing Practices Conference.

66 **Every drug is a triangle with three faces—representing the healing it can bring, the hazards it can inflict and the economic impact of each.** 99

—Jerry Avorn, *Prescription Medicines: The Benefits, Risks, and Costs of Prescription Drugs.*

Prescription drugs encompass any medication that requires a legal written order by a doctor. They are used to treat everything from mild infections such as ear infections or tonsillitis to deadly diseases such as cancer or AIDS. Some patients take prescription drugs for years to manage ongoing medical conditions such as hyperactivity or depression. Others take them to address conditions that increase the risk of a major health problem such as high cholesterol, high blood pressure, obesity, or low bone density. Other prescription drugs are taken for a much shorter period to treat a specific illness or medical problem. Most Americans have been prescribed antibiotics to help them fight a bacterial infection or have taken prescription pain relievers following surgery or an injury.

Some prescription drugs are recognizable by their chemical compound, but most are better known by the name under which they are sold. Drugs to treat high cholesterol are among the most widely prescribed drugs; retail sales in 2007 were $18.4 billion. Drugs that treat ulcers and reduce gastric acid in the stomach had prescription sales of $14.1 billion. Other classes that had sales over $10 billion include antipsychotic drugs to treat mental illnesses, antidepressants, and drugs that treat schizophrenia.

Prevalence

In the United States today, over 3 billion prescriptions for medications are filled each year—adding up to a total bill of $285.5 billion in 2007. About half of American adults take at least one prescription drug daily, and 19 percent take four or more drugs regularly.

By all accounts the use of prescription drugs is on the rise. Sales grew 3.8 percent in 2007. More people are using more drugs for more purposes than ever before. As the population ages and new drugs are discovered, the demand for drugs is likely to continue to rise.

Do Americans Take Too Many Drugs?

Patients seem to feel better just by having a prescription in their hand, and doctors tend to give them what they want. But prescription drugs can do more harm than good. Too often, antibiotics are prescribed for a viral infection, despite the fact that these drugs have no impact on viruses. Health-care advocates worry that overprescribing antibiotics can make bacteria more resistant, resulting in more serious infections in the future.

Some people also take prescription drugs to prevent a risk that is so small as to be negligible. Bone-building drugs have been developed to help treat osteoporosis, a disease common among older women that makes bones prone to facture. While older Americans with low bone density benefit from these drugs, they are sometimes unnecessarily prescribed to young women who are not at risk.

Taking more drugs than necessary jeopardizes one's health. The more drugs a person takes, the greater the risk of adverse side effects. In addition, a person's tolerance to a drug can build up over time, decreasing the drug's benefits and increasing the risk of addiction and dependency. With some drugs, such as antibiotics, health-care professionals advise that overuse can weaken one's own natural immune system.

Some people blame drug companies for encouraging people to take more drugs than they need. Drug advertisements make drugs appealing, they say. "In the last thirty years, the big pharmaceutical companies have transformed themselves into marketing machines selling dangerous medicines as if they were Coca-Cola or Cadillacs," writes Melody Petersen in a new book. "They pitch drugs with video games and soft cuddly toys for children; promote them in churches and subways, at NASCAR races and state fairs. They've become experts at promoting fear of disease, just so they can sell us hope."[1]

Benefits of Prescription Drugs

There is no doubt that drugs save countless lives and reduce the pain of living for millions more. Antibiotics have reduced many once life-threatening diseases to a minor inconvenience. Since the mid-1990s, when researchers developed drugs to treat HIV/AIDS, the U.S. death rate from AIDS dropped about 70 percent. Drugs that treat high blood pressure reduce the risk of stroke by 35 to 40 percent and of heart attack by about 25 to 30 percent. In patients with cardiac disease, drugs that lower cholesterol reduce the risk of heart attack by 20 to 30 percent and of stroke (in patients under 70) by about 17 percent. Bone-strengthening medications can help cut in half the risk of a hip fracture among high-risk patients.

> **As the population ages and new drugs are discovered, the demand for drugs is likely to continue to rise.**

Other prescription drugs make it possible for ill people to lead normal lives. Prescription pain relievers help people recover from serious injuries. Antipsychotic medications help mentally ill patients live outside of mental institutions.

Gains continue to be made for those suffering from life's many ailments. American pharmaceutical companies are testing more than 1,000 new medicines for Alzheimer's disease, stroke, cystic fibrosis, arthritis, and many other diseases. For cancer alone, there are almost 600 new medicines being tested.

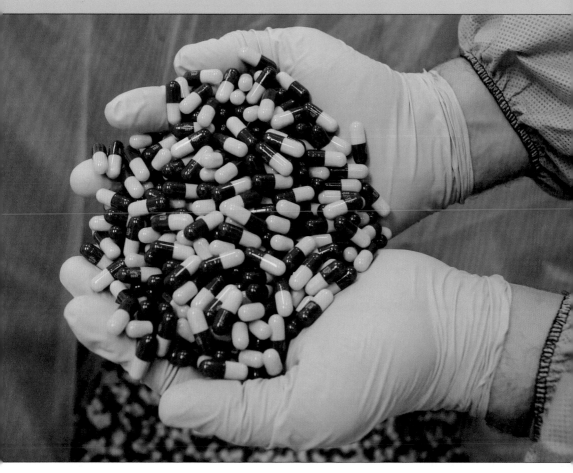

Cymbalta, an antipsychotic medication, helps mentally ill patients live outside of mental institutions. Antipsychotic drugs had sales over $10 billion in 2007.

How Do Prescription Drugs Differ from Over-the-Counter Drugs?

The main difference between prescription and over-the-counter (OTC) drugs, such as aspirin or cold remedies, is in the doses that can be taken safely. Prescription drugs typically are more addictive and have more potential side effects than OTC drugs. As a rule OTC drugs are used to treat less severe medical conditions that do not necessarily require a doctor's care.

The distinction between prescription and OTC drugs is not always clear. Dozens of drugs that were once available only with a prescription are now sold over the counter. More than 700 products sold over the counter today use ingredients or dosage strengths available only by prescription 30 years ago. OTC medications that were once only available with a prescription include ibuprofen (Advil and Motrin), allergy medications such as Benadryl and Sudafed, and drugs to treat heartburn, including Tagamet and Zantac 75. With some drugs, such as ibuprofen, a lower dosage is available over the counter, while higher dosages require a prescription.

Regulating Drug Safety and Effectiveness

Prior to the twentieth century, there were no requirements for drug manufacturers to conduct research or to prove that a drug was safe. Usually the only proof that a doctor or patient had of a drug's effectiveness was the manufacturer's assurance and/or testimonials from those who had used the drug. The first legislation regulating drugs for medical use was the 1906 Food and Drug Act, which required manufacturers to list the ingredients of a drug on its label. Government oversight was enhanced in 1938 with the Federal Food, Drug and Cosmetic Act. This law was passed after 100 deaths resulted when a chemical compound to treat bacterial infections was mixed with a toxic solvent. For the first time, the federal government required drug manufacturers to demonstrate the safety of new drugs before they could be sold to consumers.

> " American pharmaceutical companies are testing more than 1,000 new medicines for Alzheimer's disease, stroke, cystic fibrosis, arthritis, and many other diseases. For cancer alone, there are almost 600 new medicines being tested. "

Still, there was no guarantee that the drugs Americans purchased were effective until 1962, when Congress passed the Kefauver-Harris Drug Amendments. Following this legislation the FDA enlisted the National Academy of Sciences to evaluate the effectiveness of 4,000 drugs. By 1984, 1,051 of the 3,443 drugs researched had been pulled from the market because the NAS concluded that they did not have any impact on the illness or disease they proposed to treat.

The Role of the FDA

The primary responsibility for overseeing the safety and effectiveness of prescription drugs falls to the U.S. Food and Drug Administration (FDA). The FDA serves as the consumer watchdog for roughly 11,000 drugs on the market.

All drugs must receive FDA approval before coming to market. As part of this process, the FDA reviews how the drug is manufactured, its potential side effects, and the results of animal testing and clinical trials. The FDA also oversees the manufacturing, labeling, and advertising of drugs as part of its efforts to monitor their safety after approval.

Are Prescription Drugs Safe?

Most Americans assume that FDA oversight protects them from any risk to their health. In a 2008 poll 78 percent said that they are at least "somewhat" confident that prescription drugs sold in the United States are safe. Over a quarter indicated that they are "very" confident. Still, experts caution it is impossible to predict all the side effects or potential impacts of any given drug, particularly since not all drugs work the same in all populations.

It is not easy to determine how many people have died due to an adverse reaction to a prescription drug. When a person dies of a heart attack, for example, determining whether it was a drug that caused it is nearly impossible. Some experts estimate, however, that prescribed drugs are responsible for over 100,000 deaths each year. In *Death by Prescription*, Ray D. Strand cautions, "An adverse drug reaction is five times more likely to kill you than an automobile accident or AIDS."[2]

How Drugs Affect Different People

After a drug is taken, it is absorbed into the bloodstream, which carries the drug throughout the body. The drug circulates to organs and tissues. The drug is then carried to the liver, which breaks it down and flushes it away. How long drugs stay in the body—and how long they keep producing their effects—depends on how quickly the drug is broken down and removed. This process is called metabolism. Most drug metabolism takes place in the liver, where enzymes break apart the chemical compound. Metabolism also occurs in the kidneys, lungs, and stomach.

In young children and seniors, the liver and other organs function less effectively, so they do not metabolize drugs as they do in an average adult. People who are ill might also not have the same liver function as those who are healthy. This can make these populations more sensitive to a drug and its side effects. Some drugs also have been shown to have different impacts on different segments of the population—women versus men or people of different races, for instance. The federal government has responded with stricter guidelines to assess medication responses in both genders and to analyze data by age, gender, and race.

> How long drugs stay in the body—and how long they keep producing their effects—depends on how quickly the drug is broken down and removed.

In addition, the same drug can have a greater or lesser effect on people depending on how much they have eaten, what other drugs they are taking, their general health, and a host of other factors. The intake of food, for instance, can reduce the speed and extent of drug absorption, while diarrhea reduces the opportunity for a drug to be absorbed. Alcohol, herbal remedies, and even some foods also can have an impact on the effectiveness of a prescription drug.

Prescription Drug Information

The FDA requires information to be supplied to all patients who are provided with prescription medications. Most prescription drugs come with a package insert that provides detailed product information, including potential risks and side effects. The information is intended to protect patients from unintentional misuse. But the package inserts are also aimed at protecting the manufacturer from lawsuits. As a result most manufacturers list every possible problem that might occur. Some medical professionals claim that the extensive cautions on the packets might scare off some patients from taking a much-needed drug. Pharmacists are required by law to provide patients with information about a prescription drug as it is dispensed. The law allows consumers to decline this right, however. Today most pharmacies simply ask consumers who do not want to speak to the pharmacist to sign a statement to that effect.

Advertising

In 1997 the FDA relaxed its rules about direct-to-consumer (DTC) advertising for prescription drugs. Since then the amount spent on advertising has steadily increased. Manufacturers spent roughly $4.4 billion on DTC ads in 2005—up from $788 million in 1997. Advertising has a direct effect on the sale of prescription drugs—as it does with any other product. In a study done by the U.S. General Accounting Office, the number of prescriptions for the most advertised drugs rose 25 percent but increased only 4 percent for other drugs.

The pharmaceutical industry argues that such advertising is a good way to tell people about drugs and their benefits. All such ads are checked by the FDA to ensure that they are truthful. And drug makers say that responsible advertising provides a service as people demand more information for making health-care decisions.

Critics of direct advertising for prescription drugs argue that it moves the decision-making power from a doctor, who is focused on a patient's health, to the drug manufacturer, whose primary goal is making money. By promoting the use of the new, expensive drugs rather than alternatives that are already on the market, they say, advertising increases health-care costs.

Despite FDA oversight, there remain concerns about the reliability of the advertising. A *Consumer Reports* analysis of the regulatory letters that the FDA posted on its Web site from January 1997 through September 2005 concluded that "consumer-drug ads have contained a wide range of misleading messages: minimizing the risks, exaggerating the efficacy, misstating or omitting the labeling information, making false superiority claims, and promoting unapproved uses for an approved drug."[3] In 2007 3 former executives of Purdue Pharma, the maker of the blockbuster prescription painkiller OxyContin, pleaded guilty to criminal charges that the company had misled doctors and

> " In 1997 the FDA relaxed its rules about direct-to-consumer (DTC) advertising for prescription drugs. Since then the amount spent on advertising has steadily increased. "

patients when it claimed the drug was less likely to be abused than traditional narcotics. The manufacturer was ordered to pay $634.5 million—the largest penalty ever paid by a drug company in such a case.

Do Drugs Cost Too Much?

Prescription drugs amount to roughly 10 percent of America's total health-care costs. Many people say the drugs cost too much. Not all insurance companies pay for drug coverage, and an estimated 45 million Americans do not have any health insurance. In a 2008 survey 16 percent of respondents indicated that paying for drugs is a "serious problem." The cost of drugs is a particular problem for elderly people on fixed incomes. Many elderly people take several different drugs daily to manage their health.

> A number of public and private organizations use a variety of media—television ads, print material, and the Internet—to inform young people of the harmful consequences of prescription drugs.

Growing concerns about the affordability of needed drugs are causing policy makers to consider new approaches to maintaining drug costs. In 2006 prescription drug coverage was included in Medicare, the nation's health insurance for elderly citizens. Several public and private organizations provide financial assistance or free drugs to those in need. Laws currently prohibit people from importing their drugs from pharmacies in other countries, where the price is often lower. Some lawmakers argue these laws should be overturned.

How Widespread Is Prescription Drug Abuse?

Prescription drug abuse is defined as the use of a prescription medication in any way that is different from the instructions given by the doctor and/or printed on the label. According to the National Institute on Drug Abuse (NIDA), an estimated 48 million people ages 12 and older—roughly 20 percent of the U.S. population—have used prescription drugs for nonmedical reasons. This makes prescription drugs the second

This woman, 71, figures she has saved more than $10,000 in the last four years by buying her drugs in Canada. Canada has price controls for prescription drugs. In the United States, a drug's price is determined primarily by what the market will bear.

most widely used illegal substances—behind marijuana and ahead of cocaine, heroin, and barbiturates.

According to the Drug Abuse Warning Network, almost 600,000 people were taken to emergency rooms following the nonmedical use of prescription or over-the-counter drugs in 2005. This represents a 21 percent increase over the previous year.

Why Do People Abuse Prescription Drugs?

There are many reasons why people abuse prescription medications. Some people take prescription drugs because they like the "high." Teens sometimes have parties at which they take handfuls of pills, often mixed with alcohol. Some people take depressants to help them come down from the high of other illicit drugs.

But getting high is just one reason why people abuse prescription drugs. The National Youth Anti-Drug Media Campaign, an initiative that encourages youths to stay drug-free, provides other reasons for the increase in prescription drug abuse: "Teens often say they want to relieve personal or family-related stress; escape boredom; preserve friendships or romantic relationships, and compete for college admission," explains the National Youth Anti-Drug Media Campaign.[4]

When one high school student overheard her parents saying that her brother's medication for attention deficit hyperactivity disorder (ADHD) was making him less hungry, she decided to see if it could help her lose weight. She started sneaking a few of his pills every few days and asked a friend with the same prescription to sell her a few more.

How Can Prescription Drug Abuse and Misuse Be Stopped?

Preventing prescription drug abuse requires combating its root causes. Education about the dangers of prescription drugs is a key piece of any prevention strategy. A number of public and private organizations use a variety of media—television ads, print material, and the Internet—to inform young people of the harmful consequences of prescription drugs. The Partnership for a Drug-Free America, for example, operates a Web site that includes multimedia activities designed to influence the attitudes and behaviors of young people.

Other efforts focus on making it more difficult for people to get drugs without a prescription. The Drug Enforcement Administration (DEA), for instance, has targeted the illegal use of OxyContin as part of its war on drugs. The agency's efforts have led to the arrest and indictment of hundreds of doctors, pharmacists, and patients.

Prognosis for the Future

Government organizations, schools, and the medical profession are coming together to address the growing abuse of prescription drugs. Many of the same strategies that people believe have been instrumental in decreasing the use of illicit street drugs are being applied to prescription drug abuse.

Some people contend that increasing abuse of prescription drugs is a natural outgrowth of the growing number of drugs prescribed to treat pain, ADHD, and other ongoing medical problems. Doctors must constantly balance the benefits of medications appropriately used by patients against the risk that they will be used inappropriately. Meanwhile, additional studies are needed to foster prevention and intervention efforts that successfully target at-risk populations and to develop specific treatment programs for prescription drug addiction.

How Safe Are Prescription Drugs?

66Although there is always room for improvement in patient safety, the United States has the world's best drug safety record.99

—Pharmaceutical Research and Manufacturers of America, "Key Facts."

66Each day innocent citizens die at the hands of Big Pharma—oftentimes while the FDA hides known risks and condones the very drugs that cause harm—all in the name of profit at the expense of human health.99

—Byron Richards, "Dietary Supplements Threatened, Freedom in Danger."

Immediately after receiving FDA approval for Vioxx in 1999, manufacturer Merck embarked on an aggressive sales campaign. In television commercials and magazine articles, the manufacturer promised that this pill would ease the pain of osteoarthritis, a degenerative joint disease that affects many older people. The promotional campaign worked as well as the drug. By 2001 Vioxx had become one of the nation's 10 best-selling drugs, earning $2.6 billion in revenues.

Behind the scenes, however, the picture was not so rosy. Preliminary results submitted to the FDA in March 2000 showed that patients who took Vioxx suffered from twice as many heart attacks as those who did not take the drug. Although Merck continued to try to put a positive spin on these findings, the FDA was growing concerned about the drug's safety. Still, it took five years before the manufacturer conceded the drug's serious safety issues. In September 2004, under pressure from the FDA, Merck voluntarily pulled the drug from the market.

During the drug's 5 years on the market, over 20 million people had taken the drug. An FDA study linked the drug to 27,785 heart attacks and sudden cardiac deaths. Some scientists put the damage much higher, claiming that over 100,000 people had suffered Vioxx-induced heart attacks.

Reaching FDA Approval

The primary responsibility for ensuring the safety of prescription drugs falls to the FDA. The FDA does not test new drugs on its own, but instead relies on manufacturers to conduct these tests. Critics contend that it would be preferable to have a more objective review process. Derek Bok, the president of Harvard University, is among the critics of industry-supported drug studies. According to Bok, "Clinical trials supported by industry are much more likely to arrive at conclusions favorable to their sponsors than independently funded work on the same drugs."[5]

It once took the FDA an average of 30 months to review a new medication before it could be sold to the public, but this period has been greatly reduced since the enactment of the Prescription Drug User Fee Act (PDUFA) in 1992. Under the provisions of the act, drug manufacturers pay an application fee to the FDA for each proposed drug. Manufacturers also have the option of paying for priority review for innovative, life-saving drugs. Since the PDUFA, roughly 40 percent of the drugs reviewed by the FDA have been granted priority status.

> " The primary responsibility for ensuring the safety of prescription drugs falls to the FDA. The FDA does not test new drugs on its own, but instead relies on manufacturers to conduct these tests. "

Should More Testing Be Required?

Experts disagree about the amount of testing that should be required before a drug can be sold to consumers. Clinical trials usually focus on relatively healthy populations that suffer only from the illness or disease that the drug is intended to treat. This leaves a void in the information about how a drug will affect other groups of people. For instance, elderly patients are typically excluded from these clinical trials because they are more likely to have health issues that would confuse the data. In addition, doctors typically have little or no information about how a new drug will interact with other drugs on the market, increasing the risk of a dangerous drug interaction.

Yet requiring additional trials and studies would cost millions of dollars and add years to the drug discovery process. Some people say that adding the time would do little to improve a drug's safety. In the meantime, some people might die of a disease the drug could have prevented or treated.

Monitoring Drugs on the Market

Because all potential reactions to a drug cannot be determined during clinical trials, the FDA also monitors drugs that have already entered the market. "The role of our post-marketing safety system is to detect serious unexpected adverse events and take definitive action when needed," explains Steven Galson, the director of the FDA's Center for Drug Evaluation and Research.[6] In 1993 the FDA instituted MedWatch, a voluntary system that makes it easier for doctors and patients to report adverse events. In addition to relying on Med-Watch, the Center for Drug Evaluation and Research requires ongoing reporting from drug companies.

Critics contend that few drug companies report adverse reactions, even when studies clearly reveal that problems exist. Drug companies are naturally hesitant to publish results that might reflect negatively on one of their new products. A 2006 article based on research conduct-

> " Experts disagree about the amount of testing that should be required before a drug can be sold to consumers. "

ed by *Consumer Reports* concluded, "Some companies have withheld publication of studies that found serious risks, or have failed to conduct post-approval studies that they promised to the FDA."[7]

In the aftermath of Vioxx's market withdrawal, the executives of manufacturer Merck have been accused of suppressing information about the link between Vioxx and heart attacks. Similar accusations were cast at manufacturers of antidepressants in the first decade of the twenty-first century, after the FDA required manufacturers to add a warning to these drugs' labels.

> A 'black box' warning highlights serious problems that have been found with the drug's use. These warnings typically address a specific risk that has come to light since the drug was approved.

Drug companies stress that they are in the business to save lives, not put patients at risk. "Sometimes a company may not want to show data that are negative till they really know what's going on," says Marianne J. Legato, a professor of clinical medicine at Columbia University College of Physicians and Surgeons in New York City. "But it's ridiculous to suggest that they would suppress things willy-nilly, because if a drug is going to cause severe side effects, it's not in their best interest to hide that."[8] In fact, the public backlash after the integrity of drug makers was questioned following the withdrawal of Vioxx and several other major drugs caused stock prices of several drug companies to tumble and sales of their drugs to fall off.

Warnings and Market Withdrawal

If the FDA finds that a drug has adverse effects, it can order the manufacturer to change the label to include a warning about these potential problems. A "black box" warning highlights serious problems that have been found with the drug's use. These warnings typically address a specific risk that has come to light since the drug was approved. In response to the growing number of reports of OxyContin abuse, for instance, the FDA required the manufacturer to add a black box warning about the potential for abuse and addiction. A 2007 *New England Journal of Medicine* article reports that 20 percent of prescription drugs receive black box warnings after approval.

In situations in which the FDA determines that the risks of a prescription drug outweigh its benefits, the FDA can demand the drug be withdrawn from the market. Once-successful drugs that have been withdrawn from the market in recent years include Bextra and Vioxx, painkillers for osteoarthritis; fen-phen, an appetite suppressant; Rezulin, an anti-diabetic drug; and Seldane, an allergy medication.

> **Some drugs are used more for off-label purposes than for treating the diseases or symptoms that are listed on the label.**

Roughly 4 percent of drugs are ultimately withdrawn from the market for safety reasons. While people disagree about whether this suggests a good or bad safety record, a greater concern involves the amount of time it takes before the dangers of these drugs are uncovered. Only half of the drugs withdrawn from the market between 1975 and 2000 were withdrawn within 2 years of being introduced. It took almost 13 years for the antihistamine Seldane (Terfanine) to be withdrawn from the market and 10.5 years for the withdrawal of Astemizole, another antihistamine. Even when withdrawal of a drug happens quickly, often millions of people have taken it by the time it is withdrawn, because pharmaceutical companies tend to market their new drugs heavily. An estimated 20 million people had taken at least one of the five drugs withdrawn from the market between September 1997 and September 1998.

The Elderly at Risk

Drugs affect elderly people differently than younger people. With age, the liver and kidney do not function as well, so drugs are not processed in the same way. Several other organs become more sensitive to drug effects; others grow less sensitive. Relative proportions of fat and muscle change with aging, influencing the way drugs are distributed throughout the body and how long they work.

Elderly patients also tend to take more drugs over a long period of time, increasing the risk of a dangerous drug interaction. Side effects may create more problems for elderly patients as well. For instance, older patients are more likely to experience dizziness or confusion as a side effect of benzodiazepines, which are used to treat anxiety or sleep disorders. This can result in falls and serious injury.

Infants and Children

Many drugs intended for adults are prescribed to children, often in reduced dosages. Yet children have immature liver and gastrointestinal systems, so they do not metabolize drugs like adults. This can have deadly results. In 2007 a toddler in New York died after her foster mother gave her a painkiller intended for adults. Congress strengthened FDA oversight of children's medications with the Pediatric Research Equity Act of 2003.

> " Once drugs are on the market, it is up to doctors and their patients to determine whether the benefits outweigh these risks. "

Many drugs also pose a risk to fetuses, as illustrated in the thalidomide tragedy of the late 1950s and early 1960s. During this time, thalidomide was prescribed to pregnant women in many countries to ease morning sickness and to help them sleep. No one was aware of the drug's dangerous effect on the fetus. By the time these dangers came to light, more than 10,000 children were born with malformations, including underdeveloped arms and legs.

Off-Label Use

Drugs that are tested and approved for one purpose are often prescribed to treat another. In fact, this so-called off-label use accounts for an estimated 40 percent of prescription drug sales. Some drugs are used more for off-label purposes than for treating the diseases or symptoms that are listed on the label. Neurontin, for instance, was initially developed to combat epilepsy, a seizure disorder. Doctors soon learned that it could also benefit patients suffering from attention deficit disorder (ADD) and sexual dysfunction. Today an estimated 90 percent of prescriptions for Neurontin are for such off-label uses.

Health-care professionals warn that off-label use can have risks. The widespread use of a drug known as fen-phen in the 1980s provides an example of the dangers of off-label use. Fen-phen was developed and tested as a solution for obesity, but it quickly became a blockbuster diet pill. Tens of thousands of women who wanted to lose a few pounds took the drug. One of fen-phen's side effects was pulmonary hypertension, a rare but often fatal lung disease in which the blood pressure in the delicate arteries of the lungs increases to dangerous levels. By the time the FDA demanded that the drug be withdrawn from the market in September 1997, thousands of users had damaged heart valves and/or had developed pulmonary hypertension.

What Consumers Can Do

All prescription drugs carry risks. Once drugs are on the market, it is up to doctors and their patients to determine whether the benefits outweigh these risks. Enhancing the safety of prescription drugs requires education and communication between all parties. Manufacturers are required to include information about a drug and its potential risks as a package insert. In addition, pharmacists prescribing medications are required by law to provide patients with information about the drugs they are providing. Savvy patients read package information and tell their doctor or pharmacist if they are experiencing side effects.

It is also important for patients to be honest with medical professionals about their health history and drug use. Safety depends on identifying the full range of medications—both prescription and over-the-counter drugs—and herbal remedies that are used.

How Safe Are Prescription Drugs?

> **The FDA cannot be trusted to protect the public or reform itself.**

—David Graham, "Drug Safety Panel Is Criticized," *Washington Post*, June 8, 2005.

Graham, the associate director for science and medicine at the FDA, was among the first people to call attention to the dangers of Vioxx.

> **Drug safety will always be a high priority for the [FDA]. On an ongoing basis, we look for ways to improve how we communicate drug risks to the public.**

—Steven Galson, in Michelle Meadows, "Promoting Safe and Effective Drugs for 100 Years," *FDA Consumer Magazine*, January/February 2006.

Galson has served as the director of the FDA's Center for Drug Evaluation and Research since 2005.

> **It is important to realize, that 'safe' does not mean free of risk, and that there always is some risk of potential adverse reactions when using prescription drugs.**

—Sandra Kweder, Testimony before the House Subcommittee on Criminal Justice, Drug Policy and Human Resources, July 26, 2006.

Kweder is deputy director of the FDA's Office of New Drugs.

Bracketed quotes indicate conflicting positions.

* Editor's Note: While the definition of a primary source can be narrowly or broadly defined, for the purposes of Compact Research, a primary source consists of: 1) results of original research presented by an organization or researcher; 2) eyewitness accounts of events, personal experience, or work experience; 3) first-person editorials offering pundits' opinions; 4) government officials presenting political plans and/or policies; 5) representatives of organizations presenting testimony or policy.

66 If we are looking at drugs like Vioxx and Celebrex, neither should have been approved because they don't offer anything over pain relievers already sold over the counter. You don't want to accept any risk if there's no benefit over existing treatments. 99

—Marcia Angell, quoted in Daniel DeNoon, "How Safe Are America's Medicines?" WebMD Feature, May 29, 2008. www.webmd.com.

Angell is a former editor in chief of the *New England Journal of Medicine.* Her 2008 book *The Truth About Drug Companies* is highly critical of the pharmaceutical industry.

66 As a result of the combined efforts of the U.S. Food and Drug Administration (FDA) and America's pharmaceutical research companies, only about three percent of medicines have been withdrawn from the American market for safety reasons over more than 20 years. 99

—Pharmaceutical Research and Manufacturers of America, "Key Facts: U.S. Prescription Drug Safety: The Best in the World." www.phrma.org.

The Pharmaceutical Research and Manufacturers of America represents the leading pharmaceutical research and biotechnology companies in the United States.

66 Detecting, assessing, managing and communicating the risks and benefits of prescription and over-the-counter drugs is a highly complex and demanding task. [The] FDA is determined to meet this challenge by employing cutting-edge science, transparent policy and sound decisions based on the advice of the best experts in and out of the agency. 99

—Sandra Kweder, Congressional testimony regarding the safety of Vioxx, in Matthew Herper, "Face of the Year: David Graham," *Forbes*, December 13, 2004. www.forbes.com.

Kweder is deputy director of the FDA's Office of New Drugs.

❝The FDA is at war with good science, and this war is producing countless casualties among American consumers who naively believed that the FDA was trying to protect their health.❞

—Mike Adams, "Vioxx Found to Be the Single Most Dangerous Cox-2 Inhibitor Drug, Yet FDA Publicly Defends It," *Natural News*, September 13, 2006.

Adams is a consumer health advocate, author, and founder of NaturalNews.com, a Web site dedicated to the idea that the vast majority of all diseases can be prevented and even cured without drugs or surgery.

❝Requiring that drugs on the market be completely 'safe' is an impossible goal. The real question is whether a drug's dangers are in some acceptable proportion to the good it does.❞

—Jerry Avorn, *Powerful Medicines: The Benefits, Risks, and Costs of Prescription Drugs*. New York: Knopf, 2004.

Avorn is a professor of medicine at Harvard Medical School and chief of the Division of Pharmacoepidemiology and Pharmacoeconomics at Brigham and Women's Hospital.

❝The drug industry pays for almost all clinical trials of their medicines. And it is clear the companies know how to design these trials to generate data that will best sell their products.❞

—Melody Petersen, quoted in *Washington Post*, "Book World: 'Our Daily Meds: How the Pharmaceutical Companies Transformed Themselves Into Slick Marketing Machines and Hooked the Nation on Prescription Drugs'," April 3, 2008.

Petersen is an author and a former *New York Times* reporter. This quote was taken from an online interview with her following the publication of her 2008 book, which is highly critical of the pharmaceutical industry.

❝Under the PDUFA law, a lot of money is paid by the drug companies to have their drugs reviewed. There is something inherently bad about that. It doesn't smell right.❞

—Marvin M. Lipman, quoted in Daniel DeNoon, "Holes in U.S. Drug Safety Net," WebMD Health, December 5, 2005.

Lipman is the chief medical advisor for Consumers Union and emeritus professor of medicine at New York Medical College, Valhalla.

❝The pharmaceutical industry's influence gets exerted in a number of ways. One, starting [with the PDUFA], the influence was exerted by their directly funding, paying cash right up front, for FDA review. In many ways, the FDA started looking upon the industry as their client, instead of the public and the public health, which should be the client.❞

—Sidney Wolfe, "Dangerous Prescription: How Independent Is the FDA?" *Frontline*, November 13, 2003.

Wolfe has been the director of Public Citizen's Health Research Group since it was founded in 1971.

❝We [at the FDA] don't really feel pressure to please the industry. We feel quite independent among the scientists. We have a large number of mechanisms for assuring high quality of the reports that we do to make decisions about new drugs.❞

—Steven Galson, "Dangerous Prescription: How Independent Is the FDA?" *Frontline,* November 13, 2003.

Galson has served as the director of the FDA's Center for Drug Evaluation and Research since 2005.

66 The problem with the drug-safety system starts with the FDA. The agency's regulatory might has been undercut by constraints on its enforcement power, limited resources, dependency on drug-company fees to help finance the approval process, and what critics claim is a lack of will to enforce tough requirements. **99**

—ConsumerReports.org, "Prescription for Trouble: Common Drugs, Hidden Dangers," January 2006.

ConsumerReports.org is a Web site of the Consumers Union, an independent nonprofit organization whose mission is to work for a fair, just, and safe marketplace for all consumers and to empower consumers to protect themselves.

66 *Consumer Reports* implies that people at the FDA rush approvals through and don't look at safety data. But we are still the safest country in the world when it comes to drug approval. **99**

—Laurence B. Gardner, quoted in Daniel DeNoon, "Holes in U.S. Drug Safety Net," WebMD Health, December 5, 2005.

Gardner is chair of the department of medicine at the University of Miami Miller School of Medicine.

66 Drug safety monitoring is an ongoing process. It begins long before the product enters the marketplace, and continues long after it has been made available to patients. **99**

—Billy Tauzin, Pharmaceutical Research and Manufacturers Association. www.phrma.org.

Tauzin is the president of the Pharmaceutical Research and Manufacturers Association.

66 Rare adverse reactions are seldom detected by clinical trials, and they are usually only discovered years after the therapy has been adopted as routine care, as the number of patients receiving the drug increases. **99**

—Shoo K. Lee, "Re-Examining Our Approach to the Approval and Use of New Drugs," *CMAJ*, June 20, 2006.

Lee is professor of pediatrics and the scientific director of iCARE at the University of Alberta, Edmonton, Canada.

66 On a daily basis, prescription pills are estimated to kill more than 270 Americans—more than twice as many as are killed in automobile accidents. Prescription medicines, taken according to doctors' instructions, kill more Americans than either diabetes or Alzheimer's disease. 99

—Melody Petersen, *Our Daily Meds*. New York: Farrar, Straus and Giroux, 2008.

Author Melody Petersen is an outspoken critic of the pharmaceutical industry.

66 No amount of study before marketing will ever reveal everything about a new drug's effectiveness or risks. This is why post-marketing surveillance is extremely important and serves to complement the pre-marketing assessment. 99

—Sandra Kweder, quoted in Michelle Meadows, "Keeping Up with Drug Safety Information," *FDA Consumer*, May/June 2006.

Kweder is the deputy director of the Office of New Drugs in the FDA's Center for Drug Evaluation and Research.

66 Every time a physician writes a prescription, he or she must essentially weigh the inherent risk of the drug against the possible benefits for the patient. 99

—Ray D. Strand, *Death by Prescription: The Shocking Truth Behind an Overmedicated Nation*. Nashville, TN: Thomas Nelson, , 2003.

Strand is a leading authority on nutritional medicine and the author of several books on the benefits of good nutrition. His latest book is entitled *What Your Doctor Doesn't Know About Nutritional Medicine May Be Killing You.*

How Safe Are Prescription Drugs?

- **Eighty-eight percent** of Americans are confident that prescription drugs made in the United States are safe. In contrast, only **56 percent** trust the safety of drugs made in Canada and Europe, and only **14 percent** trust drugs made in China and India.

- The FDA's Center for Drug Evaluation and Research monitors the safety of roughly **11,000** prescription and over-the-counter drugs on the market.

- The FDA conducts rigorous reviews of each proposed new drug during an approval process that spans **10 to 15 years**. FDA regulators examine tens of thousands of pages of scientific data on each drug to weigh the benefits and risks of each medicine.

- In 2006 user fees paid by pharmaceutical companies accounted for **42 percent** of the budget for the FDA's Center for Drug Evaluation and Research. The percentage of the center's budget that comes from the pharmaceutical industry has increased steadily since the passage of the Prescription Drug User Fee Act in 1992.

- The FDA approved **22 new drugs** in 2006. Ten of these drugs received priority review and approval status.

- In a 2007 survey **72 percent** of respondents indicated that safety is more important than getting drugs approved as fast as possible.

Americans and Prescription Drugs

Fifty-four percent of Americans take one or more prescription drugs daily. Perhaps not surprisingly, elderly patients take the most prescription drugs: Forty-two percent of those over 65 years of age take 4 or more drugs, compared to just 2 percent of those between 18 and 29 years of age.

Percent of Americans who take prescription drugs and amount they take.

	All Adults	18–29	30–49	50–64	65 and older
No Drugs	45%	74%	58%	28%	14%
One	15%	17%	16%	14%	14%
Two	11%	4%	10%	16%	13%
Three	9%	4%	6%	12%	15%
Four or more	19%	2%	10%	29%	42%

Source: USA Today/Kaiser Family Foundation/Harvard School of Public Health, "Most Americans Take Medications, Many Can't Afford Them," 2008.

- The FDA devotes **50 percent** of its pharmaceutical review budget to safety issues.

- Fewer than **10 percent** of adverse reactions from prescription drugs are reported to the FDA.

- Of the 548 new drugs approved from 1975 to 1999, 56 (**10.2 percent**) required a new black box warning or were withdrawn from the market; 45 (**8.2 percent**) received one or more black box warnings; and 16 (**2.9 percent**) were withdrawn from the market between 1975 and 2000.

Does Speed Compromise Safety?

Some people have expressed concerns that speeding up the FDA approval process will increase the risk of having an unsafe drug on the market. The chart compares the median approval times for drugs later withdrawn from the market to those that are still being sold. It shows that faster approval times do not necessarily increase drug safety withdrawals.

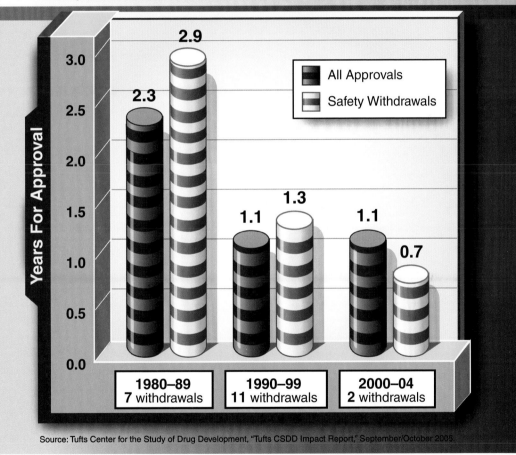

Source: Tufts Center for the Study of Drug Development, "Tufts CSDD Impact Report," September/October 2005.

- The number of drugs receiving black box warnings appears to be on the rise. The FDA issued **68 major warnings** in 2007, up from 58 in 2006 and 21 in 2003.

Prescription Drugs Pulled Off the Market

Health-care advocates raise concerns about the length of time it takes to pull a drug off the market. Some drugs are in use for years before the harms they cause are understood and the drug is taken out of circulation. This table lists drugs that were recalled between 1997 and 2003 and the length of time they were on the market before being withdrawn.

Brand Name	Approval Date	Recall Date	Recall Reason	Post Market Time
Redux	4/29/1996	9/15/1997	Abnormal Heart Valves	1.5 years
Seldane	5/08/1985	2/27/1998	Drug Interactions	12 years
Posicor	6/20/1997	6/08/1998	Sudden Deaths	1 year
Duract	7/15/1997	6/22/1998	Liver Failure	1 year
Hismanal	12/19/1998	6/18/1999	Adverse Reaction Data	6 months
Rotashield	8/31/1998	10/15/1999	Intussusception	1 year
Raxar	11/06/1997	11/01/1999	Ventricular Arrhythmias	2 years
Rezulin	1/29/1997	3/21/2000	Liver Failure	3 years
Propulsid	7/29/1997	7/14/2000	Cardiac Arrhythmias	7 years
Norplant Stytem I	12/10/1990	7/26/2000	Removal Problems	9.5 years
Lotronex	2/09/2000	11/28/2000	Constipation Problems	9 months
Raplon	8/18/1999	3/27/2001	Bronchospasm	1.5 years
Baycol	6/26/1997	8/08/2001	Rhabdomylolysis	4 years
Versed	3/18/1997	3/01/2002	Potency, Crystallization	5 years
Trovan	12/18/1997	2/28/2003	Liver Toxicity	5 years

Source: "Florida Public Health Review," 2005. http://publichealth.usf.edu.

- Statistics indicate that roughly **20 percent** of new drugs will acquire a black box warning or will be withdrawn from the market within **25 years** of being introduced.

Thousands at Risk Before Drugs Withdrawn from Market

The total number of prescriptions written for Vioxx, Celebrex, and Bextra, the three drugs in the class of compounds known as Cox-2 inhibitors, are prescribed mainly for osteoarthritis pain. Prescriptions for the best-selling drugs, Celebrex and Vioxx, began to fall off in 2001 after reports of a possible link between Vioxx and heart disease. Merck, the manufacturer of Vioxx, withdrew it from the market in September 2004; manufacturer Pfizer withdrew Bextra in April 2005 and added a boxed warning to Celebrex. Critics contend that the FDA should have acted faster and more decisively in pulling these drugs from the market.

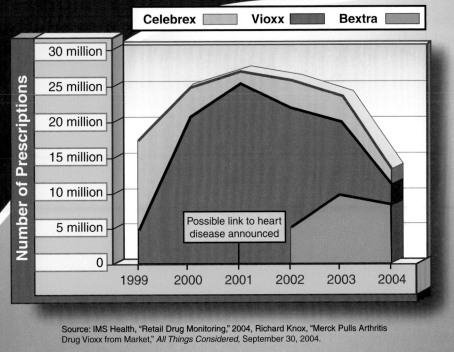

Source: IMS Health, "Retail Drug Monitoring," 2004, Richard Knox, "Merck Pulls Arthritis Drug Vioxx from Market," *All Things Considered*, September 30, 2004.

- Off-label use accounts for an estimated **40 percent** of prescription drug sales.

- One recent study showed that for each dollar we spend on medicines, we spend another dollar to treat **new health problems caused by the medicines**.

How Widespread Is Prescription Drug Abuse?

"While destructive street drugs like meth and crack produce gruesome news images and headlines, prescription drug abuse has quietly become a major part of our Nation's addiction problem."

—John P. Walters, "Federal Government Issues New Guidelines for Proper Disposal of Prescription Drugs: What Every American Can Do to Prevent Misuse of Prescription Drugs."

"Teenagers whom I interviewed said that whereas they used illicit drugs only for recreation, they often used prescription drugs for 'practical' effects: hypnotic drugs for sleep, stimulants to enhance their school performance, and tranquilizers such as benzodiazepines to decrease stress. They often characterized their use of prescription drugs as 'responsible,' 'controlled,' or 'safe.'"

—Richard A. Friedman, "The Changing Face of Teenage Drug Abuse: The Trend Toward Prescription Drugs."

When people think of prescription drug abuse, they tend to think about people taking massive amounts of pills at one time. While this is clearly drug abuse, most forms of prescription drug abuse are much less obvious. Prescription drug abuse occurs anytime a drug is used for nonmedical purposes. Any prescription medicine can be abused.

The three classes most commonly abused are opioids, which are prescribed to treat pain; stimulants, which are prescribed to treat narcolepsy and attention deficit hyperactivity disorder (ADHD); and depressants (tranquilizers and sedatives), which are used to treat anxiety and sleep disorders.

According to the 2006 National Survey on Drug Use and Health, approximately 49.8 million Americans ages 12 and older—roughly 20.3 percent of the U.S. population—have used prescription drugs for nonmedical reasons in their lifetimes. According to the National Center on Addiction and Substance Abuse, there are more prescription drug abusers in America today than cocaine, hallucinogen, inhalant, and heroin users combined.

> " Sometimes prescription drug abuse begins when people have been prescribed a drug and continue to crave it after their problem has been treated. "

Prescription drug abuse takes many forms. Some people set out to get high, using drugs that have not been prescribed to them. They might take a few pills at a party or a few tranquilizers to help them relax.

Sometimes prescription drug abuse begins when people have been prescribed a drug and continue to crave it after their problem has been treated. This is what happened in 2002 or 2003, when Santino Quaranta, the youngest player to be drafted to play professional soccer, was prescribed painkillers after an injury. Quaranta got hooked on prescription painkillers because they made him feel good. "It wasn't an instant addiction," says Quaranta. "It was on and off. I don't know when I crossed the line, but it really got bad. I was a mess."[9]

Opioids

Opioids are used to treat pain resulting from surgery or injury. In 2006 an estimated 5.2 million persons used prescription opioid painkillers for nonmedical purposes—an increase over the 4.7 million abusers in 2005 and 2.5 million in 2003. The largest increase has occurred among young adults aged 18 to 25. The most commonly abused opioids are oxycodone (OxyContin) and hydrocodone (Vicodin).

Opioids act by attaching to specific proteins called opioid receptors in the brain and spinal cord. This changes the way a person experiences pain. Opioids are often prescribed to address chronic pain. Addiction occurs when tolerance increases and the person craves the drug in greater and greater doses. According to data from the National Survey on Drug Use and Health and the National Comorbidity Survey, one in four initial users of opiates will become addicted.

OxyContin is at particular risk of abuse. Sold on the street as OC, OX, Oxy, Oxycotton, and kicker, the tablets are sometimes crushed, reversing the drug's time-release action. The pills are sometimes chewed, crushed, and snorted like cocaine, or crushed and dissolved in water and then injected like heroin. Users say that OxyContin gives the same high as heroin, but cheaper—at about one dollar per milligram. In Appalachia, where it was prescribed to manual laborers suffering from back pain or injury, the widely abused drug has become known as "hillbilly heroin." "OxyContin on the street was referred to as poor man's heroin," says a member of the Drug Task Force in Dane County, Wisconsin. "It's kind of falling into the realm now at the street level—it's just like combating cocaine, crack, heroin and everything else."[10]

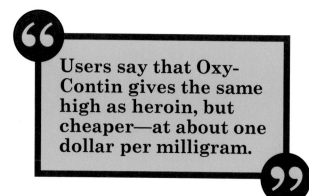

> **Users say that OxyContin gives the same high as heroin, but cheaper—at about one dollar per milligram.**

Opioid pain relievers can affect breathing. Combining opioids with alcohol, antihistamines, barbiturates, or benzodiazepines puts people at risk of respiratory arrest, a fatal event in which a person stops breathing.

Stimulants

Stimulants are prescribed to treat ADHD, a sleep disorder called narcolepsy, and obesity. According to the annual Monitoring the Future survey, an annual survey that charts drug use by eighth-, tenth-, and twelfth-grade students, 4.4 percent of twelfth graders and 4 percent of college students used stimulants without a prescription at least once in 2005. Other estimates suggest more widespread use among young people at competitive colleges and universities.

Ritalin, sometimes called "Kiddie Cocaine," "Vitamin R," or "R Ball," is the most abused stimulant among teens. Young people often obtain Ritalin from siblings, classmates, or friends who have been prescribed the drug to treat ADD or ADHD.

Many abusers believe stimulants help them focus. One person who posted anonymously on the Chronicle of Higher Education Web site said that he had become dependent on three 20-milligram doses of Adderall daily. "I'm not talking about being able to work longer hours without sleep (although that helps)," he writes. "I'm talking about being able to take on twice the responsibility, work twice as fast, write more effectively, manage better, be more attentive, devise better and more creative strategies."[11]

> " Health-care professionals warn people of the serious dangers associated with the misuse of stimulants. Stimulants act a lot like cocaine and can increase a person's heart rate and blood pressure. "

Experts caution that stimulants are not an effective study tool. "When you look at the students that use illicit [stimulants], their performance at school is worse," says Scott Teitelbaum, the medical director of the Florida Recovery Center at University of Florida. "That's probably because the need to use the drug reflects them being behind, and needing to cram and catch up."[12]

Health-care professionals warn people of the serious dangers associated with the misuse of stimulants. Stimulants act a lot like cocaine and can increase a person's heart rate and blood pressure. "What it means, in rare situations, is the person is put at risk primarily for a cardiac arrhythmia," says Lawrence Diller, author of *Running on Ritalin*. "Then there's irregular beating of the heart, which can cause sudden death."[13]

Central Nervous System Depressants

Central nervous system depressants include sedatives and tranquilizers prescribed to calm, induce sleep, or reduce anxiety. Widely prescribed depressants include Valium and Xanax. Abuse of these anti-anxiety medications can develop with prolonged use because tolerance grows relatively quickly. Increasing amounts of the drug are then needed to produce the initial effect. Some people also take these drugs to help them "come down" after taking cocaine or other recreational drugs.

Pharming

Increasingly, pharmaceutical drugs are part of teen parties. The act of swallowing handfuls of these drugs—or "pharming"—is a dangerous trend affecting younger and younger people. Steve Hayes, the director of a treatment center in the Midwest, explains:

> Some of our patients . . . tell us about parties that kids as young as 11 attend. Instead of bringing a present, each child is to bring some prescription drugs that they got from their parents' medicine cabinet. When they arrive at the party, they go into a room and pour the drugs into a punch bowl. Then the kids will take turns reaching into the bowl and taking a handful of pills. Sometimes the kids combine this with alcohol—an often lethal combination.[14]

Pharming does not always occur at parties. At one school in Texas, nine middle school students were hospitalized when a teacher reported slurred speech and sleepiness among several students who had taken prescription drugs freely offered by a student. "Somebody showed up with some [prescription drugs], a lot, and just started handing them out like candy," said the chief of police. "It was just kind of a grab bag. They didn't know what they were taking. It was a bad mistake."[15]

Populations at Risk

According to the Monitoring the Future study, prescription drug abuse among teens is on the rise. Over 11 percent of twelfth graders report that they have used prescription drugs for nonmedical reasons. Most teens try prescription drugs for the first time in high school. Only 2.7 percent of eighth graders say they have tried Vicodin, for example, compared with 9.6 percent of high school seniors.

Elderly people also are at risk of prescription drug abuse. According to the National Clearinghouse for Alcohol and Drug Information, 17 percent of adults 60 and over abuse prescription drugs. This abuse often occurs when an elderly person becomes addicted to a drug needed for a medical purpose, perhaps because he or she has not read or followed the directions on the bottle.

Another at-risk segment of the population is women. Females between the ages of 12 and 25 have shown the largest increase of prescription drug abuse over the past 2 decades. Young girls may be particularly vulnerable: NIDA reports that girls aged 12 to 14 report that painkillers and tranquilizers are among the drugs they use most to get high. Studies suggest that women are twice as likely as men to become addicted to some type of prescription drugs.

Addiction

All of the most common prescription drugs can be addictive—and opioids particularly so. As a person's tolerance to a drug increases, he or she may have to take more of the drug for the same effect. With high doses, unpleasant withdrawal symptoms may occur if the user stops taking the drug. "Every muscle in your body craves it," says Jeff Trapp, who became addicted to OxyContin after a spinal injury. "You can't sleep, can't eat. It's like the flu, but 10 times worse."[16] Another addict says simply, "The high that you think feels so wonderful quickly becomes a demon that cannot be controlled."[17]

Some addicts become so dependent on drugs that they may fake an injury or illness to obtain them. When they cannot find a doctor who will prescribe their desired drug, some people turn to dealers who sell

> **Females between the ages of 12 and 25 have shown the largest increase of prescription drug abuse over the past 2 decades.**

it on the street. Patients might turn to cocaine or heroin to get the same high. Some prescription drug abusers even resort to theft or violence to fuel their addiction. "Once patients are addicted," explains author Melody Petersen, "they change in ways that no one could have expected. Even people with families and good jobs have turned to crime to get the pills their bodies crave."[18]

Adverse Effects

The dangers of prescription drugs depend on which drugs are being abused. High doses of Xanax, for instance, have been proven to impair memory and create paranoia and suicidal thoughts. Some abusers dissolve stimulants in water and inject the drug, which can block small blood vessels and damage the lungs and retina of the eye. High doses of OxyContin and other painkillers can also cause hallucinations and insomnia. There are also dangers associated with the sudden discontinuance of high levels of depressants. Because depressants work by slowing the brain's activity, ceasing use can cause brain activity to rebound so dramatically that seizures occur.

> "When taken in high doses and/or in combination with other substances, any prescription drug can be lethal."

When taken in high doses and/or in combination with other substances, any prescription drug can be lethal. In January 2008 actor Heath Ledger died from an accidental overdose of prescription drugs. An autopsy concluded that Ledger died as the result of acute intoxication by the combined effects of oxycodone, hydrocodone, diazepam, temazepam, alprazolam, and doxylamine.

With his death, Ledger joined a long list of prescription drug overdosers—a list that includes Elvis Presley, Judy Garland, and Anna Nicole Smith. According to the Drug Abuse Warning Network, almost 600,000 people ended up in emergency rooms in 2005 due to the abuse of prescription or over-the-counter drugs. The majority of these visits (55 percent) involved multiple drugs.

Effects on Society

Prescription drug abuse does not just affect the user. In some areas the overuse and abuse of OxyContin has been blamed for sudden spikes in crime, as addicts resort to violence to get their fix. Addressing drug abuse involves all aspects of the criminal justice system, including local police, courts, and prisons.

Like alcohol and illegal substances, prescription drugs taken in high doses also can have unintended, but deadly, consequences for others.

This is particularly true when drugs are taken when driving. A 2006 national survey suggests that over 10 million Americans drove under the influence of drugs in the past year. In May 2008, 53-year-old Janene Johns was found guilty of vehicular manslaughter after she struck and killed a bicyclist in California. Johns admitted that before the accident she had taken high doses of Xanax and Ambien sleeping pills, which were prescribed weeks before the accident after the death of her husband. Statistics about the number of accidents in which prescription drugs played a role are hard to obtain, but experts contend that such incidents are a natural result of the prescription drug epidemic.

Treatment

Quitting an addiction can be tough. Treatment centers are seeing an increase in the number of prescription drug abusers who cannot quit on their own. Some of these people are ordered by a court to seek treatment when they face a criminal charge related to drug possession or drug use.

Treatment for prescription drug abuse is generally similar to treatment for other kinds of drug abuse. The focus is typically on addressing the person's addiction. This often requires slowly decreasing the drug's dose while treating withdrawal symptoms. Treatment for addiction to prescription opioids often includes methadone, a synthetic drug that blocks the effects of opioids, eliminates withdrawal symptoms, and relieves drug craving.

> On blogs and at treatment centers, former addicts share their stories of recovery. Their advice is the same: Don't start.

Behavioral strategies are often a key part of a successful treatment program. These strategies teach patients how to handle cravings, the importance of avoiding drugs and situations that could lead to drug use, and preventing and handling relapses. Therapy that helps people cope with stress can also aid recovery.

A Word to the Wise

Prescription drug addiction does not discriminate by age, gender, or race. An office worker may pop a few pills on the way to work each day to help her deal with the pressure of the job. A laborer may get hooked on pain relievers prescribed after an injury or fall. A few teens may get together to party with a handful of pills stolen from their parents' medicine cabinets. The scenarios appear very different, but over time, they can all lead to addiction and a lifelong struggle with drug dependence.

On blogs and at treatment centers, former addicts share their stories of recovery. Their advice is the same: Don't start. Parents who have lost children to addiction plead with others to watch for warning signs in their loved ones. They echo the warnings of drug prevention organizations that prescription drug abuse can be just as dangerous as more traditional illegal substances.

Primary Source Quotes*

How Widespread Is Prescription Drug Abuse?

66 Unlike illicit drug use, which shows a continuing downward trend, prescription drug abuse . . . has seen a continual rise through the 1990s and has remained stubbornly steady . . . during recent years. 99

—Nora D. Volkow, statement at a congressional hearing, March 2008.

Volkow is the director of the National Institute on Drug Abuse.

66 Prescription drugs account for the second most commonly abused category of drugs, behind marijuana and ahead of cocaine, heroin, methamphetamine, and other drugs. 99

—Office of National Drug Control Policy, "Drug Facts: Prescription Drugs," March 4, 2008.

The White House Office of National Drug Control Policy establishes policies, priorities, and objectives for the nation's drug control program.

* Editor's Note: While the definition of a primary source can be narrowly or broadly defined, for the purposes of Compact Research, a primary source consists of: 1) results of original research presented by an organization or researcher; 2) eyewitness accounts of events, personal experience, or work experience; 3) first-person editorials offering pundits' opinions; 4) government officials presenting political plans and/or policies; 5) representatives of organizations presenting testimony or policy.

"Many Americans benefit from the appropriate use of prescription painkillers, but when abused, they can be as addictive and dangerous as illegal drugs."

—Tommy Thompson, "U.S. Drug Prevention: Treatment, Enforcement Agencies Take On 'Doctor Shoppers,' 'Pill Mills,'" Office of National Drug Control Policy press release, March 1, 2004.

Thompson is the secretary of the U.S. Department of Health and Human Services.

"If you start with pills, it seems fairly sanitary and legitimate. Kids have been lulled into believing that good medicine can be used recreationally."

—Catherine Harnett, "Prescription Drugs Find Place in Teen Culture," *USA Today*, June 12, 2006.

Harnett is the chief of demand reduction for the DEA.

"Students abuse prescription drugs to get high, to self-medicate for pain episodes, to help concentrate during exam time, and to try to relieve stress. Regardless of the motivation, people need to know the risks of abuse and the dangers of mixing drugs."

—Lynda Erinoff, "Studies Identify Factors Surrounding Rise in Abuse of Prescription Drugs by College Students," *NIDA Notes*, March 2006.

Erinoff is a former member of the National Institute on Drug Abuse's Division of Epidemiology, Services and Prevention Research.

"Teens are turning away from street drugs and using prescription drugs to get high. New users of prescription drugs have caught up with new users of marijuana."

—Office of National Drug Control Policy, "Teens and Prescription Drugs," February 2007.

The Office of National Drug Control Policy establishes policies, priorities, and objectives for the nation's drug control program.

❝I don't know that many kids that have done coke, none that have tried crack, and only a few that have dropped acid. I can't even count all of the ones who've taken Adderall. In my freshman year of high school, I took it at 9 at night and stayed up all night to do math homework.❞

—Conner, quoted in Allison Stice, "Young People Taking Prescription Drug Abuse to College," March 6, 2007.

Conner is a freshman art history major at a U.S. college.

....

❝I started out taking [Fiorinal with codeine] as pre-scribed for migraine headaches, but it didn't take me long to discover that it made me feel good, made me feel like I could do anything.❞

—Leslie, "Stories of Recovery," PrescriptionDrugAddiction.com. http://prescriptiondrugaddiction.com.

Leslie is a 34-year-old woman who became addicted to prescription pain medications. She engaged in doctor shopping and other behaviors to fuel her growing dependence on the drugs before finally enrolling in a treatment center.

....

❝The first time I [took OxyContin], I was hooked. . . . Where I come from, OC is a rich boys' drug. I thought, heroin abuse, that's pretty low. I'd never stick a needle in my arm. [Eventually] I sniffed [heroin] and a week later, I was shooting. I thought I wasn't like other people doing heroin. I wasn't that low. Come to figure it out, it all leads to the same place.❞

—Paul Michaud, quoted in *USA Today*, "Prescription Drugs Find Place in Teen Culture," June 12, 2006.

Michaud is an 18-year-old who first tried OxyContin he got from a friend his freshman year of high school.

....

66 Even when the doctors gave me pills, it was just 20 or 30. I would go through those in a couple hours. I would eat 10 at a time. There weren't enough pills in the world for me. You could have put me in Iraq and I would have found a way to get pills. I should have been dead a long time ago. **99**

—Santino Quaranta, quoted in Steven Goff, "'I Should Have Been Dead': Drug Addiciton Nearly Cost United's Quaranta His Career, and More," *Washington Post*, June 21, 2008.

Quaranta is a professional soccer player, currently playing for D.C. United. His addiction to prescription painkillers nearly cost him his career.

66 There's not a day in my life as an emergency room physician that I don't have people come in seeking treatment for their addiction, having medical consequences, or overdosing. It's a widespread problem. **99**

—Wayne Pasanen, quoted in Joyce Pellino Crane, "Drug Use by Young Raises Flag," *Boston Globe*, February 5, 2006. www.boston.com.

Pasanen is the medical director of Lowell General Hospital and was the hospital's chief of emergency medicine for 30 years.

66 The vast majority of unintentional drug overdose deaths are not the result of toddlers getting into medicines or the elderly mixing up their pills. All available evidence suggests that these deaths are related to the increasing use of prescription drugs, especially opioid painkillers, among people during the working years of life. Other evidence also suggests that most of these deaths involve the misuse and abuse of prescription drugs. **99**

—Leonard J. Paulozzi, Congressional testimony on trends in unintentional poisoning, before the Senate Judiciary Subcommittee on Crime and Drugs, March 12, 2008.

Paulozzi is a medical epidemiologist in the National Center for Injury Prevention and Control division at the Centers for Disease Control and Prevention.

66 The damage to the public from these white-collared drug pushers surely exceeds the collective damage done by traditional street drug pushers. 99

—Sidney Wolfe, "Narcotic Maker Guilty of Deceit over Marketing," *New York Times*, May 11, 2007.

Wolfe is the director of the health research group at Public Citizen, an advocacy group in Washington, D.C.

66 Studies have reported that while the rates of OxyContin use have increased since 2000, the proportion of those individuals who are prescribed OxyContin and have shown signs of abuse or dependence are quite low (less than 2%). 99

—Deni Carise et al., "Prescription OxyContin Abuse Among Patients Entering Addiction Treatment," *American Journal of Psychiatry*, November 2007.

The authors of this study conclude that OxyContin is not the plague that the media has characterized it to be and that OxyContin abuse is far less likely to stem from legal prescriptions but rather as part of a broader and longer-term pattern of multiple substance abuse.

66 I lost everything when the police raided my house looking for prescription drugs. My husband and two little children were home that night. I was so ashamed I couldn't even look at them. I was arrested, put in handcuffs and locked up. My husband divorced me. My children were taken away from me. I knew I had hit bottom. 99

—A prescription drug addict, quoted in Patti Geier, "The Dark Side of Prescription Drugs," PrescriptionDrugAbuse.org. http://prescriptiondrugabuse.org.

This 44 year-old radiologist and former PTA president describes her downward spiral after becoming addicted to Vicodin.

How Widespread Is Prescription Drug Abuse?

- According to the 2006 National Survey on Drug Use and Health (NSDUH), approximately 49.8 million Americans aged 12 or older—roughly **20.3 percent**—have used a prescription drug for **non-medical** purposes.

- Pain relievers are the most abused type of prescription drugs by teens, followed by stimulants, tranquilizers. and sedatives.

- A survey of **teenagers** by the Partnership for a Drug-Free America found that one in 5 teens has taken the prescription pain reliever Vicodin, one in 10 has tried OxyContin, and one in 10 has abused Ritalin or Adderall.

- Almost two out of five teens report that they have a friend who **abuses prescription pain relievers** and nearly 3 out of 10 have friends who abuse prescription stimulants.

- Columbia's National Center on Addiction and Substance Abuse (CASA) indicates that **75 percent** of young people who take prescription drugs to get high also abuse other drugs and alcohol.

- New abusers of prescription drugs have caught up with new users of **marijuana**.

Frequency of Prescription Drug Abuse

More than one in 5 Americans has used prescription drugs for nonmedical purposes in their lifetime. People between the ages 18 and 25 are at particular risk of using prescription drugs for nonmedical purposes. Almost one-third of people in this age group say they have abused prescription drugs in their lifetime, and over 15 percent have abused drugs in the past year.

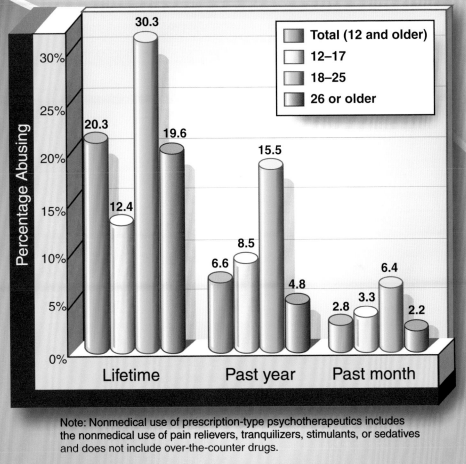

Note: Nonmedical use of prescription-type psychotherapeutics includes the nonmedical use of pain relievers, tranquilizers, stimulants, or sedatives and does not include over-the-counter drugs.

Source: SAMHSA, "National Survey on Drug Use and Health, 2006."

- **One-third** of all new abusers of prescription drugs in 2005 were 12 to 17 years old.

Prescription Drug Abuse Is Increasing

Much of the increase in prescription drug abuse can be attributed to pain relievers, particularly OxyContin. More than twice as many people reported that they had used OxyContin for non medical purposes in 2006 than in 2002.

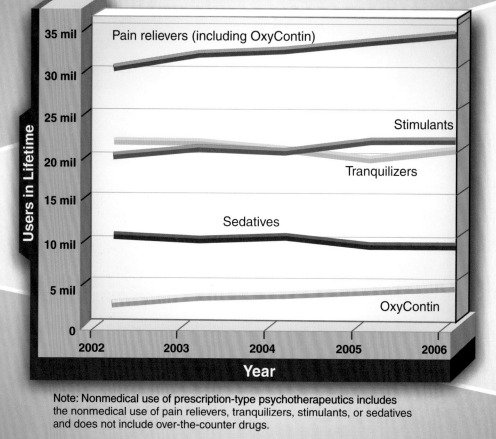

Note: Nonmedical use of prescription-type psychotherapeutics includes the nonmedical use of pain relievers, tranquilizers, stimulants, or sedatives and does not include over-the-counter drugs.

Source: SAMHSA, "National Drug Survey on Drug Use and Health, 2006."

- Prescription drugs are the **drug of choice** among 12- and 13-year-olds.

- A study by the University of Michigan Substance Abuse Research Center found that exposure to prescription pain medication early in life **increases** the likelihood of abuse in college.

- In the last 10 years, the number of teens going into treatment for addiction to prescription pain relievers has increased by more than **300 percent**.

- According to the National Clearinghouse for Alcohol and Drug Information, as many as **17 percent** of adults 60 and over abuse prescription drugs. While elderly people comprise just **13 percent** of the population, this age group represents as much as **30 percent** of the number of prescription drug abusers.

Percentage of Teens' Nonmedical Use of Prescription Drugs

This chart shows the percentage of teens in eighth, tenth, and twelfth grades who reported using prescription drugs for nonmedical purposes in the previous year. Prescription pain relievers are the most common category of drugs abused by teens. Almost one in 10 high school seniors report using Vicodin, and one of 20 has used OxyContin.

Drug	8th Grade	10th Grade	12th Grade
OxyContin	1.8%	3.9%	5.2%
Vicodin	2.7%	7.2%	9.6%
Amphetamines	4.2%	8.0%	7.5%
Ritalin	2.1%	2.8%	3.8%
Sedatives	n/a	n/a	6.2%
Tranquilizers	2.4%	5.3%	6.2%

Source: National Institute on Drug Abuse and University of Michigan, "2007 Monitoring the Future Drug Data Tables," December 2007. www.whitehousedrugpolicy.gov.

- During 2005 there were a reported **598,542** emergency room visits that involved nonmedical use of prescription or over-the-counter pharmaceuticals. Opioid pain relievers—taken alone or in combination with other drugs or alcohol—accounted for roughly one-third of all these cases.

- Emergency room visits involving abuse of prescription or over-the-counter drugs increased **21 percent** from 2004 to 2005.

- U.S. Department of Health and Human Services estimates that about **50 people a day die from drug overdoses**.

- Unintentional poisoning from prescription opioids more than doubled between 1999 and 2004 in college-age people. In 2004 there were an estimated **7,500 deaths** resulting from opioid pain relievers—more than the total number of deaths involving heroin and cocaine.

What Factors Influence Prescription Drug Costs?

> **"Prescription drugs are the best value in health care—saving lives, reducing pain and suffering, keeping people out of hospitals and nursing homes, and reducing other forms of health care spending."**
>
> —Pharmaceutical Research and Manufacturers of America, "Issues: Prescription Drug Costs."

> **"While the American people get sicker, the drug companies, insurance companies and many health 'care' providers (it's really more like 'sick care providers') are rolling in cash."**
>
> —Mike Adams, "Why Michael Moore's *Sicko* Is a Health Care Documentary Every American Must See."

In February 2006 Shirley Sobolewski of Clinton, Maryland, lost her job—and with it her health insurance. "My first and foremost concern was my medications," says Sobolewski, who was taking 13 prescriptions to protect her from health risks that include diabetes, heart disease, and kidney disease. "My meds are what keep me alive."[19]

Sobolewski could not afford to continue paying for all these medications. She knew that the free samples that her doctors gave her would not last forever, so she started cutting her pills in half to make them last longer. Sobolewski knew this too could not last. Looking back, after finally getting help from an organization called the Partnership for Prescription Assistance, Sobolewski remembers the despair she felt: "After four months of rapidly deteriorating health, and a depleted supply of meds, I had to come to accept that this was going to be how I would leave this world."[20]

Unfortunately, Sobolewski is not alone. In a 2008 poll 36 percent said they did not fill a prescription in the past 2 years because of the cost. Thirty-four percent said that they have cut pills in half or skipped doses in order to make a medication last longer.

Prescription Drug Sales Growth

The drug industry is one of the most profitable sectors of the U.S. economy. Over the past several years, sales of prescription drugs have grown by over 15 percent. That is about twice the rate of increase in overall health-care spending and 5 times the rate of inflation. In 2006 the rate of growth of drug sales slowed for the first time in many years, in part due to concerns about safety and rising prices.

The industry has done well in part because Americans are using prescription drugs to treat more illnesses than ever before. The growth of the industry also has been influenced by the demand for new, name-brand drugs that are replacing older, cheaper alternatives.

Many people worry about the amount Americans spend on drugs, but some health-care professionals argue that this is a wise investment in our future health. Prescription drugs, they say, will reduce our overall health-care cost by addressing long-term health problems and reducing the risk of a more expensive catastrophic event such as a heart attack or stroke. In addition, aggressive drug therapy for AIDS or cancer patients means that these patients spend less time in the hospital. One writer sums it up by saying, "When it comes to drugs, we're spending more and we're getting more."[21]

> Because the manufacturer of a generic drug does not have the expense of developing and testing the compound, generics can generally be sold at much lower prices than name brands.

Patents

Patents are an important factor in drug prices. Drug manufacturers obtain patents for the chemical compounds and products they develop. A patent gives the manufacturer the exclusive right to sell the drug for 20 years. During this time no other company can offer the same drug.

Patents are intended to help a drug company recoup the investment it has made in developing a new drug. It takes roughly 10 to 15 years and $800 million to bring a new drug to market. Only 30 percent of drugs that make it to market recover the cost of development for the company.

Generics

When the patent expires, other companies can make and sell the same drug. These are known as generic drugs. A generic drug has the same chemical compound as the name-brand drug.

Because the manufacturer of a generic drug does not have the expense of developing and testing the compound, generics can generally be sold at much lower prices than name brands. According to 2007 figures, the average price of a generic drug prescription is roughly $17 a prescription, versus $68 for a name-brand drug. But the price of generic drugs can vary considerably from one pharmacy to another. In 2005 a Detroit reporter found that a one-month supply of fluoxetine HCl, a generic antidepressant with the same chemical formula as Prozac, varied in retail price from a high of $92.24 to a low of $9.69.

Private Insurance Drug Benefits

Most health insurers offer a prescription drug benefit. Historically, patients enrolled in these programs pay a flat fee of $10 or $25 for each prescription. The patient's portion of the expense is called a copayment, or copay. The pharmacy is reimbursed by the insurance company for the remaining cost.

Faced with the growing cost of prescription drugs, health insurers and employers have looked for ways to control costs. Many have increased the amount of the patient's copay. They have also put caps on the total amount an enrollee can spend on prescription drugs or excluded from coverage some categories of drugs, such as newer "experimental" drugs. Prescription drug benefit managers also identify a few drugs to cover for each type of illness or disease and negotiate lower prices for these drugs.

Insurance companies may require patients to use generic drugs or charge patients the difference if they choose a brand name.

Some Americans say they are unable to pay for the drugs they need. The National Patient Advocate Foundation, which helps people who are struggling to pay medical bills, found that 31 percent of the 44,729 people it helped in 2007 said that drug copayments were the main reason they had gotten into debt. Drugs can be an overwhelming expense for people who need them to treat an ongoing illness or disease.

> **Some studies show that Americans pay more than twice the amount for the same drug as people in Canada, England, or most of Europe.**

Prescription drug costs can be especially problematic for those without health insurance. According to the U.S. Census, nearly 45 million Americans were uninsured in 2005. Ironically, people without insurance often pay more for a prescription drug than the insurance companies do, because insurers negotiate lower prices.

Medicare Part D Prescription Drug Program

Medicare is a government health insurance program covering individuals over 65 and the disabled. To address concerns about the ability of elderly citizens to afford prescription drugs, the Medicare program was expanded in 2006 to include a prescription drug benefit. This is often referred to as Part D coverage.

Medicare Part D makes prescription drug coverage available to Medicare recipients, regardless of income, health status, or prescription drug needs. Department of Health and Human Services data show that as of January 16, 2007, approximately 90 percent of all Medicare beneficiaries had drug coverage.

There are many different plans, all of which are provided by private insurance companies. Most plans charge a monthly premium (an average of $27.93), a deductible ($275 in 2008), and a small copay for each drug. Some low-income people qualify for extra help paying their costs.

In 2006 those with annual incomes of less than $6,000 were exempt from monthly premiums and deductibles.

Issues Related to Medicare Part D

While Medicare Part D has made it easier for seniors to afford drugs, there remain several issues to be addressed. A main criticism of Medicare Part D is that there are so many different plans that it is almost impossible for people to figure out which plan is best for them. A number of resources have emerged to help. A government Web site, Medicare.org, for instance, helps Medicare recipients compare plans and enroll in the one they have selected.

The existing law also prohibits the federal government from negotiating prices on behalf of Medicare patients. During the first year of the program, Part D drug prices increased several times faster than the rate of inflation. In a 2007 analysis Families USA found that the lowest price for every one of the 15 drugs most frequently prescribed to seniors increased, and the median increase was 9.2 percent. The study concludes, "For many seniors, especially those with limited incomes who depend on Social Security, Part D drugs are becoming less affordable."[22]

Why Do Drugs Cost More in the United States?

The prices of name-brand prescription medications in the United States are usually higher than in other countries. Some studies show that Americans pay more than twice the amount for the same drug as people in Canada, England, or most of Europe.

The reason for the difference in the cost of prescription drugs is that other countries have a very different health-care system than the United States. Canada and other countries have price controls for prescription drugs. In the United States, a drug's price is determined primarily by what the market will bear.

Not all prescription drugs are cheaper in other countries, however. Gener-

> **Although many Americans want to be able to buy drugs wherever they can get the best price, safety is a concern.**

ic drugs tend to cost *more* in Canada and other countries than in the United States. "Because there are so many companies in the United States that step in to make drugs once their patents expire, and because the price competition among those firms is so fierce, generic drugs here are among the cheapest in the world," explains author Malcolm Gladwell.[23]

Buying Drugs Abroad

To take advantage of the lower prices elsewhere, many Americans are defying U.S. laws that prohibit them from importing drugs from other countries. An estimated 2 million Americans buy their medicines from Canadian pharmacies over the Internet. In addition, patients—many of whom are sick or elderly—routinely travel by bus for several hours to a drugstore in Canada to have their prescriptions filled. The Minnesota Senior Federation, for instance, runs a program to help seniors import prescriptions from Canada and has organized bus trips for seniors to pharmacies in Canada for about a decade. Louisiana, North Dakota, Minnesota, Wisconsin, California, Massachusetts, New Hampshire, Maine, Illinois, and Maryland have all attempted to reimport prescription drugs; the governor of Wisconsin recently posted an online prescription drug resource center that identifies Canadian pharmacies that offer a lower price.

> **Drugs are expensive. It costs millions of dollars to find new treatments for illnesses and diseases, and companies are unlikely to invest this money unless they can sell their drugs at a profit to recoup their costs.**

There is growing controversy over whether it should be legal for Americans to purchase drugs from other countries. Although many Americans want to be able to buy drugs wherever they can get the best price, safety is a concern. Leaders within the FDA have explained that the agency cannot ensure the safety of drugs sold in other countries. For instance, the government stresses that it cannot enforce U.S. laws in other countries. There is no way to be sure that a manufacturer in another country has listed all the ingredients on the label or that a foreign pharmacy has filled a prescription as written.

Helping Patients Manage Prescription Drug Costs

A number of public and private organizations provide information and support for people who struggle to pay for drugs. Many states have Web sites that publish drug prices offered by local pharmacies and/or legitimate Internet pharmacies so that citizens can find the best price. Resources also have emerged to help people know whether they can trust an online pharmacy. PharmacyChecker.com, for instance, collects information on online pharmacies and verifies that a site is, or fills orders with, a licensed pharmacy.

People who cannot afford medications are sometimes eligible for public or private assistance. All of the major drug companies provide drugs free of charge or at reduced rates to people who cannot afford them. Organizations such as the Partnership for Prescription Assistance (PPA) help identify such resources for patients who qualify for assistance. The PPA offers a single point of access to more than 475 public and private patient assistance programs, including more than 180 programs offered by drug companies.

Will High Costs Continue?

Drugs are expensive. It costs millions of dollars to find new treatments for illnesses and diseases, and companies are unlikely to invest this money unless they can sell their drugs at a profit to recoup their costs. Americans pay handsomely for the benefit of having life-saving and life-enhancing drugs at their disposal.

As with most products, whether the price charged for drugs is too high probably depends on whether you are buying or selling the drug. Still, for patients and families—and for insurers—prescription drug expenses can add up fast.

As prescription drug costs have increased, the plight of Americans has not gone undetected. Adding prescription drug coverage to Medicare has alleviated the problem for thousands of older Americans. Public and private organizations have stepped in to help the uninsured and others who cannot afford the drugs they need. As the issue of health care remains on the forefront of the American political agenda, new approaches to affordable drugs are likely to be proposed.

What Factors Influence Prescription Drug Costs?

> **Drug prices do not just affect seniors and other consumers. They drive up costs for responsible businesses who offer workplace health benefits.**

—Center for American Progress, "Prescription Drug Reimportation: The Law & Its Problems," February 24, 2004.

Founded in 2003, the Center for American Progress is a think tank designed to provide long-term leadership and support to the progressive movement.

> **If we focus too much on cutting the cost of medicines without recognizing the growing role that medicines play in creating affordable health care, we may lose sight of their value and jeopardize future pharmaceutical research and development.**

—Pharmaceutical Research and Manufacturers of America, "What Goes into the Cost of Prescription Drugs? . . . and Other Questions About Your Medicines," June 2005.

The Pharmaceutical Research and Manufacturers of America represents the leading pharmaceutical research and biotechnology companies in the United States.

Bracketed quotes indicate conflicting positions.

* Editor's Note: While the definition of a primary source can be narrowly or broadly defined, for the purposes of Compact Research, a primary source consists of: 1) results of original research presented by an organization or researcher; 2) eyewitness accounts of events, personal experience, or work experience; 3) first-person editorials offering pundits' opinions; 4) government officials presenting political plans and/or policies; 5) representatives of organizations presenting testimony or policy.

"Drug expenditures are rising rapidly in the United States not so much because we're being charged more for prescription drugs but because more people are taking more medications in more expensive combinations."

—Malcolm Gladwell, "High Prices: How to Think About Prescription Drugs," *New Yorker*, October 25, 2004.

Gladwell has been a staff writer for the *New Yorker* since 1996. He has written two books as well as myriad articles on a wide range of social and health issues.

"High-price new drugs may be the cheapest weapon we have in our ongoing struggle against rising overall medical expenses."

—J.D. Kleinke, "The Price of Progress: Prescription Drugs in the Health Care Market," *Health Affairs,* September/October 2001.

Kleinke is a medical economist, author, and the chair and CEO of Omnimedix Institute, a nonprofit health information technology research company that he founded in 2004.

"The share of drugs in future medical spending is likely to increase sharply. But even without full cures, drugs that greatly delay the onset and severity of major diseases will reduce expensive and unproductive time spent in hospitals, nursing homes, and under the care of family members."

—Gary S. Becker, "New Drugs Cut Costs, and Medicare Can Help," *Business Week,* March 22, 2004.

Becker is a professor at the University of Chicago and a 1992 Nobel Laureate.

"American consumers often pay twice for their prescription drugs—first to the U.S. government in the form of taxes spent on research, then to drug makers holding lucrative patents."

—Katherine Greider, "Once Should Be Enough," *AARP Bulletin*, May 2006.

Greider is an outspoken critic of drug companies, charging that their success has been at the expense of American consumers. Her book, *The Big Fix: How the Pharmaceutical Industry Rips Off American Consumers*, accuses drug makers of charging exorbitant prices, with Americans footing the bill.

66 **The United States Congress must have the courage to do what the rest of the industrialized world has done and tell the industry that they may no longer corner our sick and dying into an isolated, monopolized market and force them to pay outrageous prices for their medicines.** 99

—Bernie Sanders, quoted in Patrick Leahy, "Leahy and Sanders Call for Greater Access to Reimported Prescription Drugs," United States Senator Patrick Leahy. http://leahy.senate.gov.

Sanders is an Independent representing Vermont in the U.S. Senate. In addition to supporting legislation to allow the reimportation of prescription drugs, Sanders has led bus trips of Vermont citizens to Canadian pharmacies.

66 **Many Americans are forced to take chances with their health, simply because they cannot afford the costs of modern medicines.** 99

—Ed Whitfield, "On the Issues: Prescription Drugs," United States Representative Ed Whitfield. http://whitfield.house.gov.

Whitfield is a Democrat representing the state of Kentucky in the U.S. House of Representatives. He has introduced legislation that would create a federal grant program to help establish or improve state-run prescription drug monitoring programs.

66 **During my own quest for affordable medications, I broke federal laws, I groveled, and I misused drug samples.** 99

—Emily Forest, "Beg, Borrow, or Steal: A Search for Affordable Prescription Drugs," Student Doctor Network, January 5, 2008. www.studentdoctor.net.

Forest, a staff writer for the Student Doctor Network, writes of her quest to find affordable psychotropic drugs after she reached the $2,500 prescription-drug cap on her insurance.

66Why do we care how much Prozac costs, or whether it has gone up by five or ten or even fifty percent in the past quarter? No doctor in his right mind should be prescribing it, no insurer ought to be reimbursing for it, and no patient ought to be taking it when the same drug [a generic] is available for a quarter of the cost.99

—Malcolm Gladwell, Gladwell.com, June 21, 2006. www.gladwell.com.

Gladwell has been a staff writer for the *New Yorker* since 1996. He has written two books as well as myriad articles on a wide range of social and health issues.

66The fact is, we are paying the highest prices for brand-name prescription drugs in the world and that's not fair. Let's make the global economy work for everybody.99

—Byron Dorgan, "Health Highlights," *Forbes*, May 4, 2007. www.forbes.com.

Dorgan, a Democratic senator from North Dakota, has sponsored legislation to allow the reimportation of prescription drugs.

66When Americans import medicines illegally or buy medicines online from unreliable sources, they are faced with a dangerous buyer-beware situation.99

—Lester Crawford, quoted in Michelle Meadows, "Saving Money on Prescription Drugs," *FDA Consumer Magazine*, September/October, 2005.

Crawford advocated greater use of generic drugs to counter the high cost of prescription medications during his short tenure as FDA commissioner.

66 The cost of creating a single new medication runs into hundreds of millions of dollars. . . . If those hundreds of millions of dollars are not paid for, don't expect people to keep investing that kind of money to develop new drugs to deal with cancer, AIDS, Alzheimer's, and all the other afflictions of human beings. 99

—Thomas Sowell, "Prescription Drug Politics," *Human Events*, June 30, 2003.

Sowell is a senior fellow at the Hoover Institution and author of *Basic Economics: A Citizen's Guide to the Economy*.

66 The drug companies promote myths about allegedly high research and development costs to justify the high price of prescription drugs. And, the industry exploits loopholes in the law to prevent lower price generic drugs from reaching the market. 99

—The State PIRG Consumer Protection, "Prescription Drugs: Negotiation, Reimportation, Buying Pools, and Other Important Reforms." www.PIRG.org.

U.S. PIRG, the federation of state Public Interest Research Groups (PIRGs), takes on powerful interests on behalf of the American public, working to win concrete results for our health and our well-being.

Facts and Illustrations

What Factors Influence Prescription Drug Costs?

- Drug manufacturers are among the most profitable sectors of the American economy. In 2006 they ranked second with profits of **19.6 percent** compared to **6.3 percent** for all Fortune 500 firms.

- Americans spent roughly **$286.5 billion** in 2007 on prescription drugs. Global prescription sales were **$712 billion**.

- The cost of prescription drugs accounts for over **10 percent** of America's overall health-care costs.

- From 1994 to 2005 the average annual number of prescriptions people purchased from pharmacies increased **71 percent**—from 7.9 in 1994 to 12.4 in 2005.

- Prescription drug prices increased at an average rate of **7.4 percent** in 2007. The average price of prescription drugs increased **7.5 percent** a year from 1994 to 2006—almost triple the average annual inflation rate of **2.6 percent**.

- Roughly **78 percent** of the revenue from the sale of a prescription drug goes back to the manufacturer.

Cost of Prescription Drugs Outpacing Inflation

Manufacturers of brand-name prescription drugs have been raising the prices they charge at a far greater rate than inflation. In 2006, prescription drugs increased an average of 6.2 percent–almost twice the rate of inflation.

— general inflation

▭ prescription drug prices

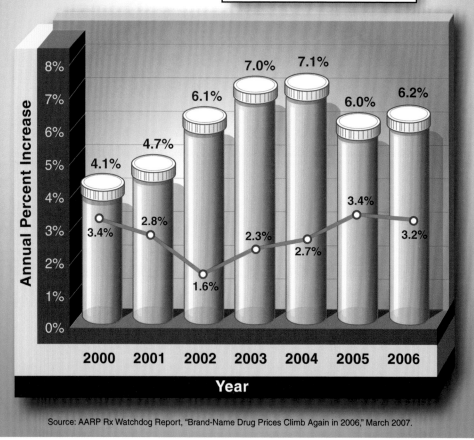

Source: AARP Rx Watchdog Report, "Brand-Name Drug Prices Climb Again in 2006," March 2007.

- Finding a new drug is expensive. It takes roughly 10 to 15 years and over **$800 million** to develop a new drug. Only one of every 10,000 compounds studied in a lab makes it to market.

Some Americans Struggle with Drug Costs

Patients do not always take drugs as prescribed. More than one-third of Americans have not filled a prescription over the past two years because of its cost and/or cut a pill in half or skipped doses to make a medicine last longer. Those who make less money are apt to engage in such cost-cutting activities.

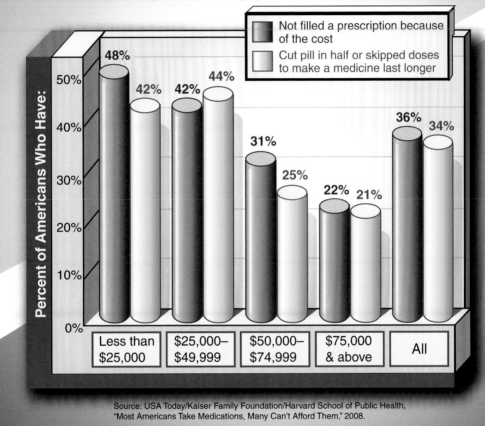

Source: USA Today/Kaiser Family Foundation/Harvard School of Public Health, "Most Americans Take Medications, Many Can't Afford Them," 2008.

- American drug makers develop and produce **75 percent** of the world's drugs. Industry-wide research and investment reached a record $58.8 billion in 2007.

- A 2008 study revealed that **80 percent** of Americans believe that the cost of prescription drugs is unreasonable, and **70 percent** feel that drug companies are too concerned about making profits and not concerned enough about helping people.

Who Pays for Prescription Drugs?

Private insurers pick up the largest portion of the prescription drug bill, but Americans pay roughly 22 percent of the cost out of their pockets. Medicare began providing prescription drug coverage for seniors in 2006 prior to this less than 2 percent of the cost of prescriptions were covered by Medicare. As the cost of prescription drugs rises, insurers and consumers will continue to feel the pinch.

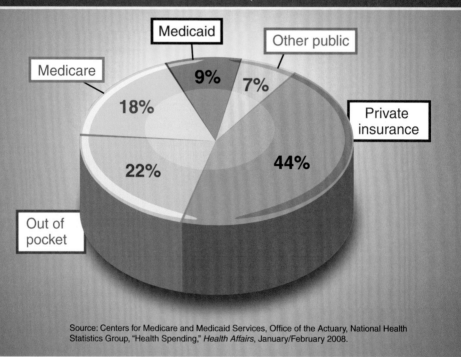

Medicaid
Other public
Medicare
18%
9%
7%
Private insurance
22%
44%
Out of pocket

Source: Centers for Medicare and Medicaid Services, Office of the Actuary, National Health Statistics Group, "Health Spending," *Health Affairs*, January/February 2008.

- Copayments have risen most sharply for costly types of drugs. Patient payments for generic drugs rose **38 percent** from 2000 to 2007, and some brand-name drugs rose **48 percent**. Inflation rose **21 percent** during those years.

- Approximately three-quarters of FDA-approved drugs have generic counterparts. In 2007 generic drugs made up more than **67 percent** of all prescription drug sales.

Women More Likely to Abuse Prescription Drugs

While men abuse drugs more than women, these gender differences are reversed when it comes to prescription drugs. Females accounted for just 35 percent of the emergency room visits in which street drugs were involved, but 55 percent of those resulting from prescription drugs.

Emergency department visits for all illegal drugs

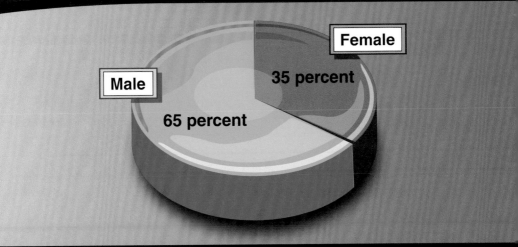

Female
35 percent

Male
65 percent

Emergency department visits for prescription drug abuse

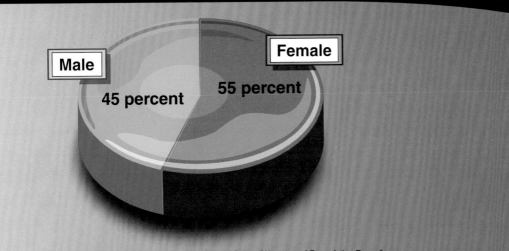

Female
55 percent

Male
45 percent

Source: Office of National Drug Control Policy, "Women and Prescription Drugs," April 2007. www.whitehousedrugpolicy.gov.

- The Congressional Budget Office estimates that consumers save nearly **$10 billion** a year by using generic drugs.

- Americans spend roughly **$700 million** each year on prescription drugs imported from Canada through Internet sales and travel to Canadian pharmacies. An additional **$700 million** of drugs is estimated to enter the United States from the rest of the world.

- The Medicare Prescription Drug Improvement and Modernization Act of 2003 established a voluntary Medicare outpatient prescription drug benefit (known as Part D), effective January 1, 2006.

- More than **3 million seniors** are falling into the doughnut hole—Medicare's prescription drug coverage gap.

How Can Prescription Drug Abuse and Misuse Be Stopped?

> **"Prescription drug abuse poses a unique challenge because of the need to balance prevention, education, and enforcement with the need for legitimate access to controlled substance prescription drugs."**
>
> —Office of National Drug Control Policy, "Drug Facts: Prescription Drugs."

> **"Drug abuse, in all its forms, is a societal issue that demands societal solutions. By engaging health professionals, families, and support groups we can provide assistance to people of all ages and from all walks of life who may be at risk, and help those who have already fallen victim to an addiction recover."**
>
> —Former U.S. surgeon general Richard H. Carmona, Office of National Drug Control Policy.

Addressing prescription drug abuse requires an understanding of its causes. Americans take more prescription drugs than ever before. With so many prescriptions for so many drugs, many people assume that they are safe, regardless of whether or not they have a prescription for them. If you are in pain or need to relax, the rationale goes, pop a pill. In one recent survey, 40 percent of teens agreed that prescription medications are much safer to use than illegal drugs. This attitude contributes to the overuse and abuse of prescription drugs.

Regardless of whether it is a high school student sharing a few pills with a sibling or a doctor selling prescriptions for profit, giving or selling a prescription drug to someone without a prescription is against the law. Throughout the country, local police have joined with the federal government to strengthen the enforcement of these laws.

Sharing Prescriptions

The majority of prescription drug abusers get their drugs from a friend or relative. High school students looking for a high often have to look no further than their parents' medicine cabinet. Eric, an 18-year-old who lives in San Francisco, says, "I can get prescription drugs from different places and don't ever have to see a doctor. I have friends whose parents are pill addicts, and we 'borrow' from them. Other times I have friends who have ailments who get lots of pills and sell them for cheap."[24]

> **Regardless of whether it is a high school student sharing a few pills with a sibling or a doctor selling prescriptions for profit, giving or selling a prescription drug to someone without a prescription is against the law.**

On college campuses, some students sell their prescription stimulants at a great profit. One recent survey showed that one in four kids with prescriptions for ADD/ADHD drugs has been approached by another teen who wanted to buy pills from them.

Doctor Shopping

To get a higher dosage of drugs than any one doctor would typically prescribe, patients—or people posing as patients—sometimes see several physicians. This practice is referred to as "doctor shopping." Perhaps the most highly publicized incident of doctor shopping involved the 2003 arrest of Rush Limbaugh, a conservative talk show host. Limbaugh allegedly obtained over 2,000 prescription narcotics over a six-month period.

Although doctor shopping is illegal in most states, the law is hard to enforce. Pain management clinics often require patients to sign an oath that they will not obtain prescriptions elsewhere, but some people say that addicts ignore their promise. "When you're addicted to drugs, you're going to do whatever you have to do to get that drug," says a police officer in Austin, Texas. "And if it means you're going to go to the next doctor and sign the same piece of paper, then you're going to do that."[25]

Pill Mills

In 2007 CBS News sent four people into a Houston medical clinic that they believed was operating outside the law. In each case the people posing as patients were able to obtain a prescription for Vicodin, Xanax, and Soma, without providing medical records or evidence that they had a medical problem. In fact, the patients never even saw a doctor. The prescription was faxed to a nearby pharmacy after the "patient" asked for it.

> " Drug traffickers often obtain prescriptions from unwitting doctors and then sell them on the street. "

Such "pill mills," as they are known, often run for years without being investigated. "These guys are very, very good at staying under the radar," says Andrea Trescot, a leading pain specialist. "It is a huge societal problem. What they're causing are patients to get addicted and potentially die."[26]

It is even more difficult to detect Internet pill mills—pharmacies that dispense drugs without a prescription. Because computer technology makes it possible for new Web sites to go up, move, and/or be taken down quickly, it is extremely difficult to track sites that are selling prescription drugs illegally.

The Supply Chain

As the demand for prescription drugs has increased, so too has the number of illegal drug rings supplying this demand. Drug traffickers often obtain prescriptions from unwitting doctors and then sell them on the street. One such dealer paid homeless people in California to pose as patients and then resold the narcotics they obtained at great profit. Drug seekers sometimes fool doctors into prescribing painkillers for weeks or

> **Stopping prescription drug abuse before it starts is a top priority in many drug control efforts. Prevention programs often include an educational and awareness aspect focusing on the dangers of these drugs.**

months by claiming they have medical conditions or ailments that are hard to diagnose, such as toothaches or kidney pain.

A growing number of interstate distribution chains are emerging, mirroring the supply chains of other illicit drugs. A 2002 DEA report described one such operation. In Tucson, Arizona, one man took advantage of a severe medical condition to obtain legitimate prescriptions for OxyContin and other oxycodone products from several different physicians and then filled the prescriptions at various pharmacies. The tablets, approximately 8,000 to 9,000 over the course of a year, were sent via FedEx to another individual in Maryland, who then sold them on the street at a substantial profit.

Theft and Forgery

Some prescription drug abusers resort to theft, stealing the drugs they want from pharmacies, doctor offices, hospitals, and other health facilities. Home burglaries may also occur when an abuser knows of someone who has been prescribed a drug that sells well on the street. The number of violent crimes, including armed robberies, associated with prescription drugs is also increasing all across the country.

In Pinellas County, Florida, for instance, police investigated just 3 pharmacy robberies between 2002 and 2004, and 15 between 2005 and 2007. To combat the problem, pharmacies are joining RxPatrol, a national database established in 2004 as a collaborative effort between law enforcement, drug makers, and pharmacies. The purpose of the database is to collect and analyze information that can assist law enforcement investigations of pharmacy crimes.

Some criminals forge prescriptions to obtain drugs illegally. Some people have been convicted of altering a legitimate prescription by increasing the amount on the prescripton or the number of refills. Others forge the prescription pads themselves, using a counterfeiter's skills to recreate the look of a legal prescription. In another scheme, the drug seeker steals the information needed from a doctor's office to con a pharmacist into believing that he or she is a doctor or an authorized member of a doctor's staff.

Education and Awareness

Stopping prescription drug abuse before it starts is a top priority in many drug control efforts. Prevention programs often include an educational and awareness aspect focusing on the dangers of these drugs. Recognizing the particular risk of adolescents, outreach programs often target high school and university students.

Materials also target parents, who may not be as vigilant about prescription drug use as cocaine or other illegal substances. Parental disapproval can have a profound impact on a teen's decision about drug use. However, research shows that less than one-third of parents have discussed prescription drug abuse with their teens.

Doctors also play a key role in addressing prescription drug abuse, whether of teens or adults. NIDA recommends that physicians ask patients at annual check-ups about substance abuse, current use of prescription and OTC medications, and the reasons patients are taking these drugs.

> " In January 2008 the Office of National Drug Control Policy (ONDCP) launched its first major federal effort to educate parents about the risks facing their children and what to look for. "

Media Campaigns

While education and awareness programs that seek to prevent prescription drug abuse come in many forms, most use some form of media to spread antidrug messages. In January 2008 the Office of National Drug Control Policy (ONDCP) launched its first major federal effort to educate parents about the risks facing their children and what to look for. The public awareness campaign began with television advertisements.

The ads were made in collaboration with the Partnership for a Drug-Free America and were aired during the 2008 Super Bowl. This initiative also includes broadcast, print, and online advertising in newspapers and magazines across the country, as well as a strong community outreach component. For instance, the ONDCP partnered with Community AntiDrug Coalitions of America (CADCA) to create a "Strategizer" for community groups. This program includes strategies, case studies, information, and resources for initiating or enhancing a prescription drug abuse campaign in local communities.

> Governments at all levels have strengthened their law enforcement efforts to control prescription drug abuse. The DEA has targeted Internet pharmacies that dispense drugs without a prescription and doctors who over-prescribe drugs.

Of course, many other organizations are involved in educating people about the dangers of prescription drugs. One Web site shows photos of teens who have died of prescription drug overdoses. The popular media also have raised the issue. *Seventeen* is among the magazines that have run stories about the dangers of prescription drugs, giving readers information about how to resist peer pressure and get help. Antidrug messages in which characters fight addiction to prescription drugs have been woven into the story lines of several popular television programs, including *Desperate Housewives, All My Children, House,* and *Without a Trace.*

Drug Monitoring Programs

Knowing what other prescriptions a person has can help detect when a patient has been doctor shopping or has obtained a higher dosage of a drug than normal. Many larger pharmacies have databases that allow pharmacists to access a patient's prescription drug history. These databases are not interconnected, so patients can easily avoid detection by having prescriptions filled at several places. Some states are addressing the problem with drug monitoring programs that cross-reference patients, drugs, and prescribing doctors. Some of these programs are accessible only by police; others are being developed for doctors and pharmacists.

Law Enforcement

Governments at all levels have strengthened their law enforcement efforts to control prescription drug abuse. The DEA has targeted Internet pharmacies that dispense drugs without a prescription. Several major cases have been brought against these "rogue" pharmacies. In August 2007 for instance, the owner of Xpress Pharmacy Direct was sentenced to three years in prison for illegally operating an Internet pharmacy that dispensed drugs without a prescription.

In 2001 the DEA developed an action plan to combat the growing OxyContin epidemic. The DEA began to target physicians and pharmacists who were believed to be writing fraudulent prescriptions for personal use or for others who planned to sell the drugs on the street. Since then more than 5,600 physicians have been investigated, and over 450 have been prosecuted on federal drug trafficking charges. Some doctors also have been charged with manslaughter or murder after patients have overdosed on prescription medication.

> " Some experts worry that physicians may hesitate to write prescriptions for pain relievers because they fear prosecution. People in acute pain often agree that prescription pain medications can be difficult to obtain, particularly without a clear diagnosis. "

In some cases physicians are clearly breaking the law by prescribing drugs without seeing patients. In May 2008 Masoud Bamdad, a physician in California's San Fernando Valley, was indicted after an eight-month DEA investigation revealed that he was writing prescriptions for pain relievers to people whom he had not examined. Bamdad allegedly charged $100 to $300 for each prescription, generating upward of $100,000 in cash per week.

The laws that apply to illegal street drugs such as herion or cocaine also apply to prescription drugs. The situation is complicated for prescription drugs, however, because it is sometimes a fine line between legal and illegal use. Doctors who have been accused of breaking the law by overprescribing prescription painkillers, for example, may believe that they are providing proper treatment for a patient who is truly in pain.

Patients can also be caught in this confusion. The case of New Jersey resident Richard Paey provides a glimpse into the complex world of prescription drug abuse enforcement. In 1985 Paey was in a car accident. The operation on his back left him in chronic, often excruciating pain.

> **As new drugs come to market, new risks and dangers will emerge. Health-care professionals and policy makers will continue to struggle with balancing the promise of cures for those who are sick against the dangers for those who are well.**

"I felt like my legs were being dipped into a furnace," says Paey. "They were burning, and I couldn't move them. It's an intense pain that, over time, will literally drive you to suicide."[27]

Doctors could do little for him beyond prescribing painkillers, including Percocet, Vicodin, and acetaminophen with codeine. When Paey moved to Florida, he had trouble getting doctors to prescribe the drugs in the high doses he needed to manage his pain. He worked out a scheme with his former doctor in New Jersey to send him prescriptions, often without the date on them. Law enforcement officers were convinced Paey was selling the drugs and arrested him. He was convicted and sentenced to 25 years in prison for drug trafficking. Paey was pardoned in 2007 after three and a half years in jail, but his case is often used to raise questions about the impact of tough prescription drug laws on patients.

Some experts believe that physicians may be hesitant to provide patients in acute pain with adequate pain relief because they fear prosecution. Those in pain often agree that prescription pain medications can be difficult to obtain, particularly without a clear diagnosis. A 2006 survey conducted by the Stanford University Medical Center found that only 50 percent of chronic pain sufferers who had spoken to a doctor about their pain got sufficient relief.

A Look to the Future

The world of prescription drugs is an ever-changing environment. As new drugs come to market, new risks and dangers will emerge. Health-care professionals and policy makers will continue to struggle with balancing the promise of cures for those who are sick against the dangers for those who are well. The FDA, law enforcement professionals, and a host of others will have to watch out for the best interest of all Americans, while doctors and pharmacists seek the best path for individual patients.

How Can Prescription Drug Abuse and Misuse Be Stopped?

66 We must abandon the notion that abuse of controlled prescription drugs like OxyContin, Valium and Xanax is somehow safer than abuse of illegal street drugs. 99

—Joseph A. Califano Jr., "Statement by Joseph A. Califano, Jr., CASA Chairman and President, on the death of actor Heath Ledger," National Center on Addiction and Substance Abuse at Columbia University, February 6, 2008.

Califano is the chair and president of the National Center on Addiction and Substance Abuse (CASA).

66 I became a very good actress. I thought I needed these drugs [prescription tranquilizers] no matter what, even if I had to bamboozle the doctors to get them. . . . I figured I had a prescription for what I was doing, which made it okay. 99

—Lynn Ray, quoted in Michelle Meadows, "Prescription Drug Use and Abuse," *FDA Consumer*, September/October 2001.

Ray became addicted to tranquilizers after she was prescribed Xanax following the death of her infant son.

* Editor's Note: While the definition of a primary source can be narrowly or broadly defined, for the purposes of Compact Research, a primary source consists of: 1) results of original research presented by an organization or researcher; 2) eyewitness accounts of events, personal experience, or work experience; 3) first-person editorials offering pundits' opinions; 4) government officials presenting political plans and/or policies; 5) representatives of organizations presenting testimony or policy.

66 **Parents need to know that teens are turning away from street drugs and increasingly abusing prescription drugs to get high. They should also be aware that suppliers of these drugs might not be sinister characters on the street corner, but are more likely close friends or relatives. Too many young people see popping pills as a painless high.** 99

—John P. Walters, "Teens Turn Away from Street Drugs, Move to Prescription Drugs, New Report Reveals," Media Campaign press release, February 14, 2007.

Walters is the director of the White House's Office of National Drug Control Policy.

66 **The world of children and teens is awash in prescription drugs and some parents can become inadvertent drug pushers by leaving their prescription opioids, stimulants and depressants in places where their kids can get them.** 99

—Joseph A. Califano Jr., "Teens Turn Away from Street Drugs, Move to Prescription Drugs, New Report Reveals," Media Campaign press release, February 14, 2007.

Califano is the chair and president of the National Center on Addiction and Substance Abuse (CASA) at Columbia University.

66 **Parents and educators often think of drugs as using crack or meth or marijuana. They often forget that the drugs the kids have the easiest access to are right there in their own homes. Prescription drugs can be just as dangerous.** 99

—Kenneth Trump, quoted in Jennifer Radcliffe, "Students Ill After Pills Given Out 'Like Candy,'" *Houston Chronicle*, January 25, 2007.

Trump is the director of the National School Safety and Security Services.

66 **I did not know prescription-drug abuse was a problem. There's so much guilt in that. I don't know if I stuck my head in the ground. I did not see this coming.** 99

—Phil Bauer, in *USA Today*, "Prescription Drugs Find Place in Teen Culture," June 12, 2006.

Bauer's 18-year-old son died of an overdose of prescription drugs.

66 **Controlled substances are too accessible on the Internet, where instead of a prescription, all that's needed is a credit card. The results can be tragic.** 99

—Dianne Feinstein, "Senate Approves Feinstein-Sessions Bill to Stop Controlled Substances from Being Sold Online Without Valid Prescriptions," Dianne Feinstein press release, April 1, 2008.

Feinstein is a U.S. senator from California. In memory of Ryan Haight, a California high school honors student and athlete who died of an overdose of hydrocodone he purchased over the Internet, Feinstein joined with Jeff Sessions to introduce legislation to strengthen laws regulating the sale of prescription drugs over the Internet. The Senate unanimously passed the bill on April 1, 2008.

66 **Patients tell me they worked as a maid at the height of their addiction and they would go through people's medicine cabinets. I had a patient who was a roofer tell me, 'If you ever let a roofer in your house and in the bathroom, chances are they are looking through your medicine cabinet.'** 99

—Kyle Kampman, quoted in Susan J. Landers, "Dangerous Diversions: Specter of Prescription Drug Abuse Creates Tough Balancing Act for Doctors," American Medical News. www.amednews.com.

Kampman is the medical director of the Charles O'Brien Center for Addiction Treatment at the University of Pennsylvania.

66 **In response to growing concern among federal, state and local officials about the dramatic increase in the illicit availability and abuse of the prescription drug OxyContin, the Drug Enforcement Administration (DEA) has embarked on a comprehensive effort to prevent its diversion and abuse.** 99

—Drug Enforcement Administration, "Action Plan to Prevent the Diversion and Abuse of OxyContin," DEA Office of Diversion Control, February 8, 2001. www.deadiversion.usdoj.gov.

The U.S. Drug Enforcement Administration is the federal agency responsible for enforcing the controlled substances laws and regulations of the United States.

66 **Criminals who divert legal drugs into the illegal market are no different from a cocaine or heroin dealer peddling poisons on the street corner.** 99

—Karen Tandy, "U.S. Drug Prevention, Treatment, Enforcement Agencies Take On 'Doctor Shoppers,' 'Pill Mills,'" press release, Office of National Drug Control Policy, March 1, 2004.

Tandy served as the head of the DEA from 2003 until 2007.

66 **As prescription-drug abuse and criminal diversion escalates, there is a need for stepped-up law enforcement. But when it comes to managing legitimate medical practice issues, the cops should step aside.** 99

—Scott Gottlieb, "Opinion: Cops and Doctors," *Wall Street Journal*, February 27, 2008.

Gottlieb is a practicing internist in Stamford, Connecticut, and a former deputy commissioner of the FDA.

66 **There is a fine balance between under-prescribing and over-prescribing pain relievers, particularly opioids.** 99

—National Institute on Drug Abuse, "NIDA Community Drug Alert Bulletin: Prescription Drugs," October 2005.

The National Institute on Drug Abuse (NIDA), an arm of the U.S. Department of Health and Human Services, supports research into drug abuse and addiction and disseminates the results of this research.

66 **We hate to see somebody in pain run out of medicine, so sometimes we may be a little too generous.** 99

—Kyle Kampman, quoted in Susan J. Landers, "Dangerous Diversions: Specter of Prescription Drug Abuse Creates Tough Balancing Act for Doctors," American Medical News. www.amednews.com.

Kampman is the medical director of the Charles O'Brien Center for Addiction Treatment at the University of Pennsylvania.

66 Fifty million Americans are in severe pain from arthritis, back injuries, cancer and other disabilities. But the government is sending a message to avoid prescribing strong pain-killers. 99

—Scott Fishman, quoted in Margot Roosevelt, "Why Is the DEA Hounding This Doctor?" *Time*, July 18, 2005.

Fishman is the president of the American Academy of Pain Medicine and a specialist on pain management. He is the author of *War on Pain*, published in 1999.

66 Many doctors . . . have been arrested or threatened with loss of their medical licenses simply for prescribing opiate-based pain medications in doses that federal drug authorities believe are too high. 99

—Pain Relief Network, "The Politics of Pain." www.painreliefnetwork.org.

The Pain Relief Network was founded in 2002 in response to the Bush administration's crackdown on pain-treating physicians.

66 I have lost hope of retrieving my life as it was. I currently have a physician who has said that I am psychologically manufacturing my headaches, and that I am addicted to narcotic pain relief. This of course is not the first time that I have been treated as a 'nut' or a 'junkie.' 99

—Kathleen Lohrey, in a letter requesting treatment for migraines sent to William E. Hurwitz.

Lohrey is an occupational therapist and former patient of Hurwitz's. Hurwitz was tried for overprescribing opioid pain relievers. Lohrey testified on his behalf.

Facts and Illustrations

How Can Prescription Drug Abuse and Misuse Be Stopped?

- Approximately **60 percent** of prescription drug abusers get the medication from a friend or relative.

- Roughly **62 percent** of teens say prescription pain relievers are easy to get from parents' medicine cabinets; **50 percent** say they are easy to get through other people's prescriptions. **Thirty-nine percent** of 14- to 20-year-olds say it is easy to get prescription drugs online or by phone.

- One in four teens with a prescription for ADD/ADHD drugs has been approached by another teen who wanted to **buy pills** from them.

- The majority of teens (**56 percent**) agree that prescription drugs are easier to get than illegal drugs.

- In a 2007 survey of the parents of middle school students, only **6 percent** of parents said they are concerned about their children abusing prescription drugs.

- According to the 2008 National Drug Threat Assessment, **32.8 percent** of parents talked to their children about the danger of using prescription drugs without a prescription. This is fewer than the number who have discussed heroin, cocaine, crack, marijuana, and alcohol abuse.

- More than three-quarters (**78.8 percent**) of state and local law enforcement agencies report either high or moderate availability of illegally diverted pharmaceuticals.

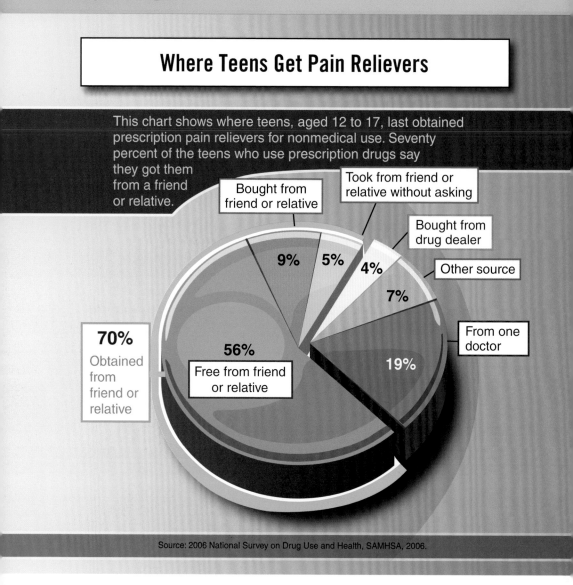

Where Teens Get Pain Relievers

This chart shows where teens, aged 12 to 17, last obtained prescription pain relievers for nonmedical use. Seventy percent of the teens who use prescription drugs say they got them from a friend or relative.

Bought from friend or relative

Took from friend or relative without asking

Bought from drug dealer

9%

5%

4%

Other source

7%

70%
Obtained from friend or relative

56%
Free from friend or relative

From one doctor

19%

Source: 2006 National Survey on Drug Use and Health, SAMHSA, 2006.

- Nationwide, **25 million** doses of commonly abused drugs were reported stolen in 2007. The majority of thefts occur at pharmacies, but prescription medicines are also stolen from medical practitioners and manufacturers.

- A 2006 study by the National Center on Addiction and Substance Abuse found that 9 out of 10 Web sites selling pharmaceuticals **did not require a prescription**.

- Since the 2001 crackdown by the DEA on the illegal trafficking of opioid painkillers, over **5,600 physicians** have been investigated on suspicion of "drug diversion," and over **450 doctors** have been prosecuted for charges ranging from illegally prescribing drugs and drug trafficking to manslaughter and murder.

States Add Prescription Drug Monitoring Programs

Prescription drug monitoring programs that provide a searchable database of prescriptions filled by pharmacies are considered to be a valuable tool in the fight against prescription drug abuse. As of January 2008, 26 states had such programs in place. Another nine have passed legislation to create such databases. Although some people believe a national database is needed, plans for such a program are not in place.

Prescription Drug Monitoring Program (PDMP) Status as of January 2008

Legend:
- Enacting enabling legislation and operational PDMP
- Enacted enabling legislation
- Pending PDMP legislation
- No legislation

Source: Office of National Drug Control Policy, "National Drug Control Strategy, 2008 Annual Report," 2008. www.whitehousedrugpolicy.gov.

Treatment for Prescription Drug Abuse on the Rise

The number of people admitted to treatment centers for abuse of or addiction to prescription drugs has increased consistently over the past decade, fueled by an increase in addiction to opiate pain relievers, including OxyContin. In just 10 years (from 1996 to 2006), the number of people admitted to treatment centers for opiate addiction more than quadrupled, from 16,605 to 74,750. In 1996, fewer than 17,000 people were admitted to treatment centers for opiate addiction; just 1.0 percent (16,605 of 1,643,731) of admissions to treatment centers for opiates; by 2006, this percentage had jumped to 4.2 percent (74,750 of 1,800,717). There were also almost twice as many admissions for tranquilizers in 2006 than in 1996, but the difference in admissions for sedatives remained relatively constant.

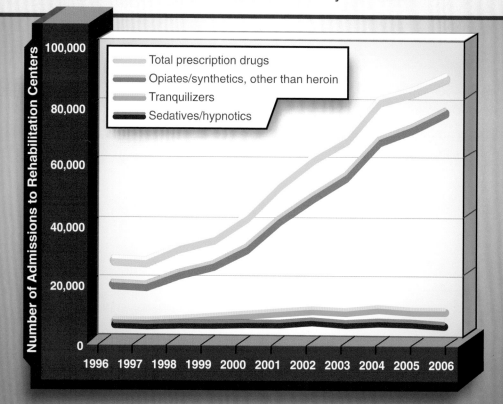

Source: Office of Applied Studies, Substance Abuse and Mental Health Services Administration, "Admissions to Substance Abuse Treatment Centers," 2007.

OxyContin and Vicodin Arrests on the Rise

As prescription drug abuse has increased, the Drug Enforcement Administration (DEA) has stepped up enforcement of illegal sales of prescription drugs, focusing particular attention on opioids, such as OxyContin and Vicodin. As shown in this chart, the number of arrests for these two drugs has increased rapidly over the past five years.

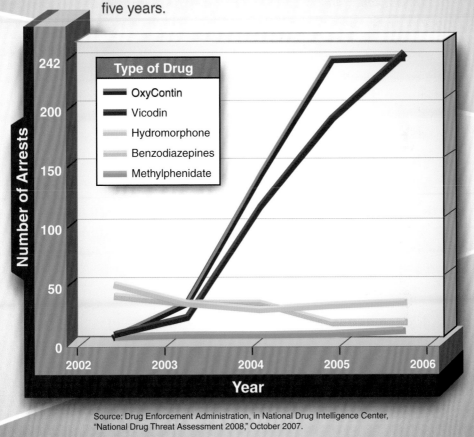

Source: Drug Enforcement Administration, in National Drug Intelligence Center, "National Drug Threat Assessment 2008," October 2007.

- A 2006 survey conducted by the Stanford University Medical Center found that only **50 percent** of chronic pain sufferers who had spoken to a doctor about their pain got sufficient relief.

Key People and Advocacy Groups

Marcia Angell: A nationally recognized authority in the field of health policy and medical ethics, Angell is an outspoken critic of the health-care system and pharmaceutical industry. Prior to joining Harvard Medical School's Department of Social Medicine, she served as editor in chief of the *New England Journal of Medicine* and has written several books on issues in American health care.

Jerry Avorn: Avorn is a professor of medicine at Harvard Medical School and chief of the Division of Pharmacoepidemiology and Pharmacoeconomics at Brigham and Women's Hospital. He is one of the nation's foremost researchers on prescription drug use, with particular reference to elderly patients and chronic disease.

David Graham: Graham is the associate director for science and medicine at the FDA. He was among the first people to call attention to the dangers of Vioxx and has been outspoken in his criticism of FDA and its relationship with the pharmaceutical industry.

Sandra Kweder: Kweder is the deputy director of the FDA's Office of New Drugs, the arm of the Center for Drug Evaluation and Research that is responsible for the review and approval of new drugs. She serves as a spokesperson for the FDA, assuring Congress and the public of the safety of our prescription drugs.

National Institute on Drug Abuse (NIDA): The institute is the arm of the U.S. Department of Health and Human Services that supports research into drug abuse and addiction and disseminates the results of this research.

Pain Relief Network: The network was formed in 2003 to oppose the federal government's crackdown on opioid pain relievers. The Pain Relief Network calls attention to the plight of people in chronic pain and their difficulties in finding treatment and works on behalf of pain physicians through lobbying and legal efforts.

Pharmaceutical Research and Manufacturers of America (PhRMA): This is the main lobbying group for pharmaceutical research and biotechnology companies in the United States. In addition to providing membership services for its members, the PhRMA issues a wide range of studies and reports on the benefits of prescription drugs.

Billy Tauzin: Tauzin is the president and chief executive officer of the PhRMA. Prior to accepting this position in 2005, he served in the U.S. House of Representatives for 25 years and played a key role in shepherding the Medicare Prescription Drug Bill through Congress. He continues to lobby on behalf of the pharmaceutical industry.

Nora Volkow: Volkow is one of the country's foremost addiction researchers and the director of the National Institute on Drug Abuse. An expert on the brain's dopamine system, Volkow has conducted extensive brain imaging studies on the effects of a number of prescription drugs and has been instrumental in demonstrating that drug addiction is a disease of the human brain.

John Walters: Walters is the director of the White House Office of National Drug Control Policy. As the nation's "drug czar," Walters oversees all federal drug programs, including the National Youth Anti-Drug Media Campaign, which partners with other organizations to reduce drug use and addiction.

Chronology

Chronology

1912
The Sherley Amendment is enacted, prohibiting manufacturers from labeling medicines with false therapeutic claims intended to defraud the purchaser, a standard difficult to prove.

1970
The Comprehensive Drug Abuse Prevention and Control Act categorizes drugs based on abuse and addiction potential compared with their therapeutic value.

1914
The Harrison Narcotic Act requires prescriptions for products exceeding the allowable limit of narcotics and mandates increased record keeping for physicians and pharmacists who dispense narcotics.

1951
The Durham-Humphrey Amendment outlines the kinds of drugs that cannot be used safely without medical supervision and restricts their sale to prescription by a licensed practitioner.

1910   **1930**   **1950**   **1970**

1906
The Food and Drug Act becomes the first legislation governing the sale of drugs. It requires drug labels to accurately identify a drug's ingredients and identity.

1937
Elixir Sulfanilamide, containing the poisonous solvent diethylene glycol, kills 107 Americans.

1960s
Thalidomide, a drug developed to treat nausea in pregnant women, causes birth defects in thousands of babies born in western Europe.

1938
The Federal Food, Drug, and Cosmetic Act gives the federal government authority to regulate the safety of drugs sold to Americans.

1962
Kefauver-Harris Drug Amendments are enacted. For the first time, drug manufacturers are required to prove to the FDA the effectiveness of their products before marketing them.

1965
Drug Abuse Control Amendments are enacted to address problems caused by abuse of depressants, stimulants, and hallucinogens.

1977

The FDA's Bioresearch Monitoring Program ensures the quality and integrity of data submitted to the FDA and increases the safety of people in clinical trials by focusing on preclinical studies on animals and clinical investigations.

2001

In response to what is perceived to be a growing epidemic, particularly in rural areas of the United States, the U.S. Drug Enforcement Administration (DEA) initiates the OxyContin Action Plan, targeting the illegal sale and use of prescription pain relievers.

2003

The Pediatric Research Equity Act requires sponsors conduct clinical research into pediatric applications for new drugs.

1992

The Prescription Drug User Fee Act requires drug and biologics manufacturers to pay fees for product applications. The act requires the FDA to use these funds to hire more reviewers.

1980

1990

2000

1984

Drug Price Competition and Patent Term Restoration permits the FDA to approve generic versions of brand-name drugs without repeating the research done to prove them safe and effective.

1993

MedWatch is launched to provide health professionals with a means to report adverse reactions to the FDA.

2004

Vioxx, a widely used osteoarthritis medicine, is withdrawn from the market after studies show a link to cardiovascular problems and heart attacks, raising concerns about FDA oversight and the safety of prescription drugs on the market.

1998

The FDA establishes new requirements for manufacturers of selected new drugs to conduct studies to assess their safety and efficacy in children.

1988

The Prescription Drug Marketing Act is passed, prohibiting the diversion of prescription drugs from legitimate commercial channels.

2006

Part D of the Medicare Prescription Drug Improvement and Modernization Act of 2003 goes into effect, providing Medicare beneficiaries with prescription drug coverage.

Related Organizations

Families USA

1201 New York Ave., Suite 1100

Washington, DC 20005

phone: (202) 628-3030 • fax: (202) 347-2417

e-mail: info@familiesusa.org

Families USA is a national nonprofit organization dedicated to the achievement of high-quality, affordable health care for all Americans. The organization engages in research, lobbying, and programmatic activities to address the affordability of health care, including prescription drugs.

Henry J. Kaiser Family Foundation

2400 Sand Hill Rd.

Menlo Park, CA 94025

phone: (650) 854-9400 • fax: (650) 854-4800

Web site: www.kff.org

The Kaiser Family Foundation is a nonprofit, private foundation dedicated to providing information and analysis on heath-care issues to policy makers, the media, the health-care community, and the general public.

National Institute on Drug Abuse (NIDA)

6001 Executive Blvd., Room 5213

Bethesda, MD 20892

phone: (301) 443-1124

e-mail: information@nida.nih.gov • Web site: www.nida.nih.gov

NIDA is part of the National Institutes of Health, a branch of the Department of Health and Human Services. It both supports and conducts extensive scientific research on drug abuse and addiction. By disseminating its research findings, NIDA hopes to prevent drug abuse, improve treatment options, and influence public policy.

Office of National Drug Control Policy (ONDCP)

PO Box 6000

Rockville, MD 20849-6000

phone: (800) 666-3332 • fax: (301) 519-5212

Web site: www.whitehousedrugpolicy.gov

The White House Office of National Drug Control Policy (ONDCP) was established by the Anti-Drug Abuse Act of 1988 to formulate and implement the nation's drug control program. The goals of the program are to reduce illicit drug use and drug-related trafficking, crime, and violence.

Pain Relief Network

518 Old Santa Fe Trail, Suite #1, Box 519

Santa FE, NM 87505

phone: (877) 473-5434 • fax: (505)995-6201

e-mail: info@painreliefnetwork.org

The Pain Relief Network was formed in 2003 to oppose the federal government's crackdown on providers of pain relief. This network of pain patients, family members of people in pain, physicians, attorneys, and activists works to ensure that people in chronic pain have access to physicians willing to treat their pain.

Partnership for a Drug-Free America

405 Lexington Ave., Suite 1601

New York, NY 10174

phone: (212) 922-1560 • fax: (212) 922-1570

Web site: www.drugfreeamerica.org

The Partnership for a Drug-Free America is a nonprofit organization that works to educate the public, particularly young people, about the dangers of drug abuse. Through extensive media campaigns, the partnership hopes to spread its antidrug message and prevent drug abuse among the nation's youth.

Pharmaceutical Research and Manufacturers of America (PhRMA)

950 F St. NW

Washington, DC 20004

phone: (202) 835-3400 • fax: (202) 835-3414

Web site: www.phrma.org

The PhRMA represents the leading pharmaceutical research and biotechnology companies in the United States.

Substance Abuse and Mental Health Services Administration (SAMSA)

1 Choke Cherry Rd.

Rockville, MD 20857

phone: (877) 726-4727 • fax: (240) 221-4292

Web site: www.samhsa.gov

This agency of the U.S. Department of Health and Human Services funds and administers a wide range of programs to address substance abuse among Americans. Through the Office of Applied Research, SAMSA also collects, analyzes, and disseminates national data on behavioral health practices and issues, including the annual National Survey on Drug Use and Health, the Drug Abuse Warning Network, and the Drug and Alcohol Services Information System.

U.S. Food and Drug Administration (FDA)

5600 Fishers Ln.

Rockville, MD 20857-0001

phone: (888) 463-6332

Web site: www.fda.gov

Situated within the U.S. Department of Health and Human Services, the FDA is the primary agency responsible for assuring the safety of human and veterinary drugs, biological products, medical devices, our nation's food supply, cosmetics, and products that emit radiation. It oversees the safety of pharmaceutical drugs through product approvals, OTC and prescription drug labeling, and drug manufacturing standards.

For Further Research

Books

John Abramson, *Overdosed America: The Broken Promise of American Medicine*. New York: HarperPerennial, 2005.

Marcia Angell, *The Truth About the Drug Companies: How They Deceive Us and What To Do About It*. New York: Random House, 2004.

Jerry Avorn, *Powerful Medicines: The Benefits, Risks, and Costs of Prescription Drugs*. New York: Knopf, 2004.

Rod Colvin, *Overcoming Prescription Drug Addiction: A Guide to Coping and Understanding*. Omaha, NE: Addicus, 2008.

————, *Prescription Drug Addiction: The Hidden Epidemic*. Omaha, NE: Addicus, 2001.

Greg Critser, *Generation Rx: How Prescription Drugs Are Altering American Lives, Minds, and Bodies*. New York: Houghton Mifflin, 2005.

Michael C. Gerald, *The Complete Idiot's Guide to Prescription Drugs*. New York: Alpha, 2006.

Merrill Goozner, *The $800 Million Pill: The Truth Behind the Cost of New Drugs*. Berkeley and Los Angeles: University of California Press, 2004.

Katherine Greider, *The Big Fix: How the Pharmaceutical Industry Rips Off American Consumers*. New York: PublicAffairs, 2003.

Barry Meier, *Pain Killer: A "Wonder" Drug's Trail of Addiction and Death*. New York: Rodale, 2003.

Cindy R. Mogil, *Swallowing a Bitter Pill: How Prescription and Over-the-Counter Drug Abuse Is Ruining Lives—My Story*. Far Hills, NJ: New Horizon, 2001.

Ray Moynihan and Alan Cassels, *Selling Sickness: How the World's Biggest Pharmaceutical Companies Are Turning Us All into Patients*. New York: Nation, 2005.

National Center on Addiction and Substance Abuse at Columbia University, *Women Under the Influence*. Baltimore: Johns Hopkins University Press, 2006.

Melody Petersen, *Our Daily Meds: How the Pharmaceutical Companies Transformed Themselves into Slick Marketing Machines and Hooked the Nation on Prescription Drugs*. New York: Farrar, Straus and Giroux, 2008.

Ray D. Strand, *Death by Prescription: The Shocking Truth Behind an Overmedicated Nation*. Nashville, TN: Thomas Nelson, 2003.

Periodicals

Julie Appleby, "As Drug Ads Surge, More Get Rx's Filled," *USA Today*, February 29, 2008.

———, "Drug Costs Rise as Economy Slides," *USA Today*, February 4, 2008.

Carol J. Boyd et al., "Adolescents' Motivations to Abuse Prescription Medication," *Pediatrics*, December 2006.

Richard Friedman, "The Changing Face of Teenage Drug Abuse: The Trend Toward Prescription Drugs," *New England Journal of Medicine*, April 6, 2006.

Richard C. Goldsworthy, Nancy C. Schwartz, and Christopher B. Mayhorn, "Beyond Abuse and Exposure: Framing the Impact of Prescription-Medication Sharing," *American Journal of Public Health*, June 2008.

Scott Gottlieb, "Opinion: Cops and Doctors," *Wall Street Journal*, February 27, 2008.

Katharine Greider, "Once Should Be Enough," *AARP Bulletin*, February 24, 2004.

Sean Hennessy and Brian L. Strom, "PDUFA Reauthorization: Drug Safety's Golden Moment of Opportunity?" *New England Journal of Medicine*, April 26, 2007.

Henry J. Kaiser Family Foundation, "Prescription Drug Sales Growth Slows to Lowest Rate Since 1961," Kaiser Daily Health Policy Report, March 13, 2008.

Karen E. Lasser et al., "Timing of New Black Box Warnings and Withdrawals for Prescription Medication," *Journal of the American Medical Association*, May 1, 2002.

Shoo K. Lee, "Re-Examining Our Approach to the Approval and Use of New Drugs," *CMAJ*, June 20, 2006.

Donna Leinwand, "Prescription Drugs Find Place in Teen Culture," *USA Today*, June 13, 2006.

Patrick L. McKercher, "Powerful Medicines: The Benefits, Risks, and Costs of Prescription Drugs," *American Journal of Health-System Pharmacy*, September 1, 2005.

Michelle Meadows, "Prescription Drug Use and Abuse," *FDA Consumer Magazine*, September/October 2001.

———, "Promoting Safe and Effective Drugs for 100 Years," *FDA Consumer Magazine*, January/February 2006.

Pharmaceutical Research and Manufacturers of America, "What Goes into the Cost of Prescription Drugs? . . . and Other Questions About Your Medicines," June 2005.

Marie Reed, "An Update on Americans' Access to Prescription Drugs," Issue Brief, Center for Studying Health System Change, May 2005.

Steven Reinberg, "Americans Confused About FDA and Drug Safety: Poll Finds Many Mistrust the Job the Agency Is Doing," *Health Day*, September 20, 2007.

Cynthia Smith, "Retail Prescription Drug Spending in the National Health Accounts," *Health Affairs*, January/February 2004.

Lori Whitten, "NIDA Notes: Studies Identify Factors Surrounding Rise in Abuse of Prescription Drugs by College Students," National Institute on Drug Abuse, n.d.

Internet Sources

Congressional Budget Office, "Research and Development in the Pharmaceutical Industry," October 2006. www.cbo.gov/ftpdocs/76xx/doc7615/10-02-DrugR-D.pdf.

ConsumerReports.org, "Prescription for Trouble: Common Drugs, Hidden Dangers," January 2006. www.consumerreports.org/cro/health-fitness/drugs-supplements/common-drugs-hidden-dangers-106/overview.

FamiliesUSA, "Out of Bounds: Rising Prescription Drug Prices for Seniors," July2003. www.familiesusa.org/assets/pdfs/Out_of_Bounds ab79.pdf.

The Henry J. Kaiser Family Foundation, "Impact of Direct-to-Consumer Advertising on Prescription Drug Spending," June 2003. www.kff.org/rxdrugs/upload/Impact-of-Direct-to-Consumer-Advertising-on-Prescription-Drug-Spending-Summary-of-Findings.pdf.

————, "Prescription Drug Trends," May 2007. www.kff.org/rxdrugs/index.cfm.

Monitoring the Future, 2007: National Results on Adolescent Drug Use, "Overview of Key Findings," National Institute on Drug Abuse. http://monitoringthefuture.org/pubs/monographs/overview2007.pdf.

National Drug Intelligence Center, *National Drug Threat Assessment 2007*. www.usdoj.gov/ndic/pubs21/21137/index.htm.

National Institute on Drug Abuse, "NIDA Community Drug Alert Bulletin: Prescription Drugs," October 2005. www.drugabuse.gov/PrescripAlert.

————, "NIDA InfoFacts: Prescription Pain and Other Medications," June 2006. www.drugabuse.gov/infofacts/PainMed.html.

————, "Research Report: Prescription Drugs: Abuse and Addiction," August 2005. www.drugabuse.gov/ResearchReports/Prescription/Prescription.html.

Office of National Drug Control Policy, Executive Office of the President, "Drug Facts: Prescription Drugs," March 4, 2008. www.whitehousedrugpolicy.gov/drugfact/prescrptn_drgs/index.html.

————, "Teens and Prescription Drugs: An Analysis of Recent Trends on the Emerging Drug Threat," February 2007. www.whitehousedrugpolicy.gov/news/press07/043007.html.

Partnership for Drug-Free America, "The Partnership Attitude Tracking Study (PATS)," 2006. www.drugfree.org/Files/Parent_with_children.

Public Citizen's Congress Watch, "America's Other Drug Problem: A Briefing Book on the Rx Drug Debate," 2003. www.citizen.org/documents/dbbapril.pdf.

Substance Abuse and Mental Health Services Administration, "Drug Abuse Warning Network, 2005: National Estimates of Drug-Related Emergency Department Visits," February 2007. http://dawninfo. samhsa.gov/files/DAWN-ED-2005-Web.pdf.

———, "Misuse of Prescription Drugs," National Survey on Drug Use and Health (NSDUH), 2006. www.oas.samhsa.gov/prescription/ toc.htm.

———, "Substance Abuse Treatment Advisory: OxyContin: Prescription Drug Abuse," April 2006. http://download.ncadi.samhsa.gov/ prevline/pdfs/MS726.pdf.

Substance Abuse and Mental Health Services Administration, Office of Applied Studies, "DASIS Report: Prescription and Over-the-Counter Drug Abuse Admissions," July 11, 2002. www.oas.samhsa.gov/2k2/ OTCtx/OTCtx.htm.

Tufts Center for the Study of Drug Development. http://csdd.tufts.org.

USA Today/Kaiser Family Foundation/Harvard School of Public Health, "The Public on Prescription Drugs and Pharmaceutical Companies," March 4, 2008. www.kff.org/kaiserpolls/pomr030408pkg.cfm.

U.S. Food and Drug Administration, "Innovation or Stagnation? Challenge and Opportunity on the Critical Path to New Medical Products," March 2004. www.fda.gov/oc/initiatives/criticalpath/white paper.html.

Source Notes

Overview

1. Melody Petersen, *Our Daily Meds: How the Pharmaceutical Companies Transformed Themselves into Slick Marketing Machines and Hooked the Nation on Prescription Drugs*. New York: Farrar, Straus and Giroux, 2008, jacket flap.
2. Ray D. Strand, *Death by Prescription: The Shocking Truth Behind an Overmedicated Nation*. Nashville, TN: Thomas Nelson, 2003.
3. ConsumerReports.org, "Misleading Drug Ads," January 2006. www.consumerreports.org.
4. Media Campaign, "Rx—A New Intentional High for Teens," February 14, 2007. www.mediacampaign.org.

How Safe Are Prescription Drugs?

5. Quoted in Jerry Avorn, *Powerful Medicines: The Benefits, Risks, and Costs of Prescription Drugs*. New York: Knopf, 2004, p. 213.
6. Quoted in Michelle Meadows, "Promoting Safe and Effective Drugs for 100 Years," *FDA Consumer Magazine*, January/February 2006. www.fda.gov.
7. ConsumerReports.org, "Prescription for Trouble: Common Drugs, Hidden Dangers," January 2006. www.consumerreports.org.
8. Quoted in Irene S. Levine, "A Dose of Reality," *Reader's Digest*, April 2005. www.rd.com.
9. Quoted in Steven Goff, "'I Should Have Been Dead': Drug Addiction Nearly Cost United's Quaranta His Career, and More," *Washington Post*, June 14, 2008, p. E5.

How Widespread Is Prescription Drug Abuse?

10. Quoted in WiscTV.com, "OxyContin: The Good, the Bad, the Deadly: Pharmacists, Police Fight to Keep OxyContin off the Streets," February 14, 2006.
11. Quoted in Benedict Carey, "Brain Enhancement Is Wrong, Right?" *New York Times Week in Review*, March 9, 2008. www.nytimes.com.
12. Quoted in News-Medical.net, "Ritalin Abuse Is on the Rise Among Teens," May 13, 2007. www.news-medical.net.
13. Quoted in Linda Ciampa, "Ritalin Abuse Scoring High on College Illegal Drug Circuit," CNN.com, January 8, 2001. http://archives.cnn.com.
14. Steve Hayes, "Teen Prescription Drug Abuse," PrescriptionReport.com, March 13, 2008. http://blog.prescriptionreport.com.
15. Quoted in Jennifer Radcliffe, "Students Ill After Pills Given Out 'Like Candy,'" *Houston Chronicle*, January 25, 2007, p. A1. www.chron.com.
16. Quoted in Nick Miroff, "A Dark Addiction," *Washington Post*, January 13, 2008, p. A1.
17. Chad, "Stories of Recovery," PrescriptionDrugAddiction.com. http://prescriptiondrugaddiction.com.
18. Petersen, *Our Daily Meds*, p. 266.

What Factors Influence Prescription Drug Costs?

19. Quoted in Sharing Miracles, "A Blog of Personal Stories of Miracles and Hope: Shirley Sobolewski." www.sharingmiracles.com.
20. Quoted in Sharing Miracles, "A Blog of Personal Stories of Miracles and Hope."

21. Malcolm Gladwell, "High Prices: How to Think About Prescription Drugs," *New Yorker*, October 25, 2004. www.newyorker.com.
22. Families USA, "Medicare Part D Prices Are Climbing Quickly," April 2007. http://familiesusa.org.
23. Gladwell, "High Prices."

How Can Prescription Drug Abuse and Misuse Be Stopped?

24. Quoted in Friedman, "The Changing Face of Teenage Drug Abuse," p. 1,448.
25. Quoted in *Austin News*, "'Doctor Shopping' a Growing Crime of Desperation," April 7, 2008. www.kxan.com.
26. Quoted in CBS News, "Inside a 'Pill Mill': CBS News Investigates the Proliferation of Clinics That Dole Out Highly Addictive Painkillers," May 31, 2007. www.cbsnews.com.
27. Quoted in *60 Minutes*, "Prisoner of Pain: How One Man's Quest for Pain Relief Landed Him in Jail," CBS News, January 25, 2006. www.cbsnews.com.

List of Illustrations

List of Illustrations

Index

About the Author

Lydia Bjornlund is a freelance writer in Northern Virginia, where she lives with her husband, Gerry Hoetmer, and their wonderful children, Jake and Sophia. She has written a dozen nonfiction books for children, mostly on American history and health-related topics. She also writes books and training materials on land conservation, public management, and industrial design for adult audiences. Bjornlund holds a master's degree in education from Harvard University and a BA from Williams College.